T0171408

GRANDPA'S CODE

BRUCE E. BRYCE, D.MIN.

WestBow
PRESS
A DIVISION OF THOMAS NELSON

WestBow Press books may be ordered through booksellers or by contacting:

WestBow Press
A Division of Thomas Nelson
1663 Liberty Drive
Bloomington, IN 47403
www.westbowpress.com
1-(866) 928-1240

Because of the dynamic nature of the Internet, any web addresses or links contained in this book may have changed since publication and may no longer be valid. The views expressed in this work are solely those of the author and do not necessarily reflect the views of the publisher, and the publisher hereby disclaims any responsibility for them.

Any people depicted in stock imagery provided by Thinkstock are models, and such images are being used for illustrative purposes only.

Certain stock imagery © Thinkstock.

ISBN: 978-1-4497-2612-6 (sc)
ISBN: 978-1-4497-2613-3 (hc)
ISBN: 978-1-4497-2611-9 (ebk)

Library of Congress Control Number: 2011915523

Printed in the United States of America

WestBow Press rev. date: 09/19/2011

DEDICATION

To Jamie, Michael, Anne, Megan, and Brian.

Life is a gift from God. He gives it to us along with a code by which to live it. The Bible is that code, and what I have written, I hope you will call "Grandpa's Code."

Your friend and mine, Frank (Saint Francis), put it to work. I hope you will follow his example. He gave me a reason to know God and helped me make sense out of a religion gone sour with complications like tradition, polity, dogmatism, provincialism and self-justification. He said: *"Lord, make me an instrument of your peace. Where there is hatred, let me sow love; Where there is doubt, faith; Where there is despair, hope; Where there is darkness, light; Where there is sadness, joy. Divine Master, let me not so much seek to be consoled as to console; not so much to be understood as to understand; not so much to be loved as to love. For it is in forgiving that we are forgiven. It is in loving that we are loved. It is in dying that we are born into eternal life.*

Amen."

CONTENTS

FOREWORD

A grandfather has the joy of bringing children into the world and, when they are grown up, watching them do the same. Most granddads don't take the time or have the opportunity to put on paper what they hope will help their grandchildren avoid their mistakes and learn from their successes. Retirement gives me an opportunity to write what I have come to believe and I sincerely hope my grandchildren will take it seriously. There are many codes that govern people's lives. The work that I have done in this book constitutes the code by which I live. To my grandchildren, I pray that *Grandpa's Code* will inspire them to create their own.

Labels bother me. They are restrictive and, more times than not, they are not completely accurate. They are the cause for stereotypes and snap judgments about a person's character and point of view. I don't think anyone is completely conservative or totally liberal or precisely moderate.

When I became a pastor more than four decades ago, I was counseled by an ecclesiastical superior to "be yourself." His wisdom has borne fruit many times over. Whenever I tried to be someone else, I usually failed and produced a second-rate facsimile of the person I wished to imitate. My friend and classmate, Fred Rogers, got a lot of mileage out of the line, "I like you as you are." He spent a considerable amount of his extremely productive career telling children that they were special just the way they were and that they didn't have to apologize for it. They were special by "just your being you."

What you will find on the following pages is the result of me being myself and not caving in to the temptation to align myself with those who would praise me because I agree with them. I try hard not to allow myself to be proud of the fact that I am part of the "right" group or the "in" way of thinking or the "correct" party or denomination or whatever group that would consider itself to be the only true group that God approves to fulfill his hopes for the world. What you will read is what I am and who I am becoming.

I built a ministry that had its foundation on the simple philosophy that I would meet people at their level of spiritual and religious need. I try not to be too dogmatic about that which I believe to be the truth. I resist judging the beliefs of others. Although I have failed more times than I should have, I always tried to overcome the tendency to put my ideas above those of someone who had a different point of view than mine. Jesus said, "Whoever would be great . . . let him be [a] minister and whosoever would be chief . . . let him be [a] servant." (Matthew 20:26 & 27) That makes sense to me. I confess to have failed in this effort but, deep down, I know how hard I have tried to live it in spite of my ego and the self-serving instincts that are so important to the successful American cleric.

What follows is my attempt to justify what has become of my life and my relationship with my God. He and I have formed a personal friendship. Even though he *is the* God my Father (Yahweh Allah Abba—Hebrew, Arabic, Aramaic), he has always been and will always be the one closest to me and most understanding of what I have thought, felt, believed and professed. His acceptance has always been the one realization that has helped me tolerate the criticisms of those who would be "correct" and who would consider me out of tune with what a person of my occupation or calling *should* think or be. The Holy Spirit of God has helped me survive long enough to become confident enough in whom and what I have become spiritually, intellectually and professionally to write what you are going to read and not worry about what *they* think.

In the spirit of what Saint Paul wrote to his pupil, Timothy, when he too approached the conclusion of his life and ministry, I am not ashamed of what you will read. I *know* whom and what I believe and am persuaded that, by his Spirit, he will help me keep that which I have committed and to which I can fervently testify. This labor of faith and love is the result of nearly seventy years of talking the talk with God and walking the walk with people. Along the way there have been many wise and friendly spirits who comprise a "great cloud of witnesses" that have walked and talked with me. If there is a God, I believe it "with all [my] heart, and all [my] soul, and with all [my] strength and with all [my] mind," and the common sense He has bestowed within me to fully love him, my neighbor and myself. I am convinced that this is an act of faith. I accept it from within the context of my personal experience, the writers of the Bible, and many other inspired works of those to whom God has revealed himself, his way and his truth. I am not ashamed to profess respect of many whose religion and theology are dissimilar from mine but whose understanding within the context of their lives is just as valid.

People like Abraham, Jacob, Moses and David, who struggled to overcome their considerable egos, have guided me in overcoming mine. Giants like Confucius, Lau Tsu, Buddha and Mohammad have broadened my understanding of the God who created the planet earth and the universe and before whom there is no other. Masters such as Jeremiah, Amos, Peter, Paul and other Bible writers have brought the context of their time profoundly into mine. Their common sense and persistent personalities never allowed the resistance of humanism and the arrogance of religion to hinder the fulfillment of God's call to them.

Brothers like Francis of Assisi, John Wesley and others like them have shown me how to overcome my lustful, covetous human nature and how to humbly approach the glory of God sans the trappings of my self. The insights of Huston Smith, Karen Armstrong, Joseph Girzone and a host of mentors have challenged my thinking. Souls like Earl Weaver, John Wells, Roland Brown and John Warman gave me courage to do that which I couldn't understand but to which God has called me. Above all, Jesus Christ, who revealed himself to me and showed me his "Way." Add to these the many parishioners, patients, friends, and "lights" that have crossed my path over the years and you will understand how indebted I am to the God who sent them to me. Together they have prompted me to resist the proud and pharisaic arrogance of those who would "know it all" and have the "only" true religion and pathway to heaven.

Last, but far from least, I thank God for the woman my grandchildren call "Nana." She was born five days after me and has been my companion and the one true love of my life for more than half a century. She is not the stereotypical "preacher's wife." In fact, she has done everything she could to resist that label. Her sometimes brutal honesty has been the bridle in my mouth and one reason I have maintained my course. Because of her, I have had the glorious experience of being a father and a grandfather and a man the community respects. Even though she has known me as I really am—and almost as well as my God—she has loved, tolerated and supported me as well as fed my body, mind and spirit with her unique and genuine personality. When it comes to me and my ego, she is far from gentle. The sharpness of her tongue and her insights have left their mark and, like the wisdom of the Psalmist, they have given me strength and quality because of the "labor and sorrow" that emanated from her being and landed on my shoulders and in my heart.

To my grandchildren I dedicate this effort. Maybe it will encourage them to build their own personal relationship with *the* God of the universe.

Introduction

Dear and beloved children,

The Bible is unique among the world's great literary works. There are other enduring religious, theological and philosophical books, but few, if any, have the universal appeal as that which contains the scriptures of the Jews and the Christians. It is the foundation for most of what your mom, your dad, Nana and I have tried to teach you about life. It is " . . . a lamp unto your feet and a light unto your pathway." (Psalm 119: 105) The Koran, the Bhagavad-Gita, the Tao Te Ching are also significant writings of other great world religions. They have influenced billions of people, but they are, for the most part, provincial. That is not to say that they are any less insightful and revealing about God to those to whom they appeal than the Bible is to the many Jews and Christians who live all over the world.

Within this catholic (universal or world-wide) faith some practitioners are labeled liberals, some conservatives. Some are called fundamentalists or traditionalists and others revisionists, reformists or moderates. There is a label for each of us, and they bother me. They are restrictive and, more times than not, they are not completely accurate. Too often they cause us to form false impressions about people who are different. Opinions about such things as race, religion, sex and nationality are often distorted by being labeled. They can freeze one's perspective with a wrong impression of someone else's character, ability or point of view. I don't think anyone is completely conservative or liberal or precisely moderate. We are what and who we are. I wish we could relate to each other without labels. Maybe then we could come to fulfill Jesus' hopes that we would love one another. (John 13:34)

It is spiritually, socially, and politically uncomfortable to straddle a doctrinal, political, philosophical or religious fence. It hurts to sit on the edge and find yourself unable or unwilling to move. But there comes a time when discomfort becomes so great that you must move one way or the other, if for no other reason than to choose the lesser of two uncomfortable positions. Like it or not, there is no way to avoid such a dilemma. You must take responsibility for what you believe, whether it is comfortable or popular or not. Likewise, to make no decision is to decide to remain on the sharp edge between the issues and that, in itself, can painfully identify who you are and what you believe as much as if you choose to accept a label that would define you and your beliefs. Accepting a label demands your time, talent, energy, economics and faith. Fence straddling is just as demanding as being on one side or the other. When you choose to sit on the fence, you are liable to be labeled indecisive and unreliable.

I call myself a "Commonsensible Contextualist." I have chosen to fashion this label for myself in order to make it clear just where I stand on issues related to my faith and religion. It gets me off the fence and into territory that I choose to inhabit. It is a label that has taken more than half a century to create. It is the result of submitting myself to the discipline of studying the points of view of many wise people who espouse many different things. It has taken me on a road on which I have considered each seriously before choosing which to accept, which to reject and which to modify to fit how I feel and what I have come to believe is right for me.

Religious beliefs are refined by human experience. Spiritual relationships with God transcend religion. Religion has been created in human minds through human institutions. Faith is built on a personal, spiritual relationship with God. I have found peace and purpose from Truth and I see Him revealed from within the common-sense context of the Bible. What I believe is also the result of digesting other divinely inspired writings as well as my experience of day-to-day living in the presence of the One who has many names. I call Him Yahweh Allah Ein Sof, which can be translated I AM The God Without End.

Religion is a means to an end, not the end in itself. That's the problem with the Church. She has too often said that if you have membership in her, you have earned eternal life. Jesus didn't teach that. He taught, "This is eternal life, that you *know* God . . ." (John 17:3)

So far I haven't needed scientific, mathematical or historical facts to verify this preference. I am not a biblical literalist. I have fashioned the term "contextualist" to satisfy just how I feel. I do not presume the declarations of the Bible to be scientifically, mathematically or historically correct. But I do believe they tell the truth, the whole truth and nothing but the truth within the context of the history of the world, God's revelation and my personal existence.

I am completely convinced that a being called Yahweh (I AM) by the Jews and Christians, Allah (The God) by the Muslims, Ein Sof (Without End) by the Kabbalists and Abba (Father) by Jesus Christ created the heavens and the earth. However, it isn't essential for me to know how he did it or how long it took him. The context of the story reveals all the truth I need to build a faith in him and establish a course for my life.

God is good enough for me to build a faith that gives meaning to the cosmos and purpose for my particular life. It is enough for me to clarify the reality of the universe, the spark of the human soul and the image in which my soul was created. I don't need to know when it began or how it evolved. However, I do concede that there are those who are interested by these puzzles and consequently must follow their inspiration to find answers that make as much difference in their lives as my answers do in mine.

Scientists will be quick to concede that they have only scratched the surface of the potential for human knowledge. There are those who will spend a lifetime seeking the origins of the universe and exploring the nature of the atom. I maintain that the common sense context of the Bible has all I need or want to satisfy my quest for knowledge and understanding. I find it comforting to realize that the effects of those whose interests are unlike mine contribute to my understanding of the context of God within the big picture of life.

Descartes said, "I think, therefore I am." I can, with equal certainty say, "I believe, therefore God exists." It is common sense that brings me to the conclusion that there is a mentality or a purpose behind the existence of all that is humanly experienced, whether it can be scientifically explained or not. Just as I accept electricity as a reality even though I cannot see it and have not the first clue as to how it works, so I accept the reality of God. Pascal said that if he believed in God, and God exists, then he had gained everything he wanted and lost nothing. He also said that if he believed in God and God did not exist, he would still have gained all that he wanted and would have lost nothing.

I trust those who understand scientific phenomenon and who have investigated its origins and components. I accept the pronouncements of science, but when it conflicts with what my common-sense faith tells me, I must wrestle with these differences and eventually yield to the truth. I believe I have a responsibility to be open to the amazing facts that mathematics, chemistry and physics reveal. I allow the reality of that which is beyond my comprehension but is evidently true. What difference is there for a guy like me to believe in a power called electricity and credit a power called God to be its originator and creator? I think those who accept the reality of electricity but deny the reality of God is inconsistent and unfaithful to the divine force of spirit that attracted them to seek an understanding of the physical universe.

The Bible has made a valid attempt to tell the truth. It was written at a time when few people could read and books didn't exist. Scientific knowledge as we know it today would have overwhelmed the minds of those who lived three millennia ago. Since they could not possibly understand what modern physics, geography, geology, astronomy, mathematics and a multitude of other space-age technologies have revealed, they needed a vehicle to give them understanding that the origin of their world had a purpose. It took a genius to inspire truth that was conveyed to people with such limited knowledge; a divine mind to fashion the right words for ignorant people to comprehend what was to become general scientific knowledge. It takes faith to accept what the Bible says and it takes common sense within the context of the physical and spiritual universe to understand why it was written.

Genesis states, "In the beginning, God created the heavens and the earth." I believe this to be the truth. What follows are details that are harmonious within the context of three millennia ago. The truth remains: God is *the* creator. The physical facts have been and will continue to be revealed for as long as there is an earth inhabited by human beings who are inquisitive as to the source (Source) of their origins.

As I write these words, I am sitting in the midst of great trees on the side of a mountain. I hear the wind blow. I ask myself, "From whence does it come?" I don't know. I don't possess the scientific understandings of its origins. I believe there are those who do and I trust their findings because they have proven themselves in the past to be reliable. But I don't care. I know that the ultimate Designer of the breeze and the symphony it plays in the trees intrigues me more than the meteorology of it. I am not saying that meteorology isn't important. But for me, that breeze draws my mind and spirit beyond the visible to the invisible God. I don't need facts to believe that God composed the symphony of sound that pleases my ears and soothes my skin. The truth that all nature works in harmony is good enough for me.

It is just common sense to believe in God. Just as there is a physical answer for electricity to be found in science and a corporal answer for the source of the breeze, so there is an answer for the reality of God. The means by which that truth is attained is called faith. As my faith makes me turn the switch on the wall that causes a light to appear and as my bodily senses confirm the presence of the breeze, so my faith tells me that at the heart of the universe is God.

Common sense within the context of human understanding is a plausible launching pad from which one can begin a search of the Bible to find Truth (God). If you want to get facts, get a physics textbook or an almanac or go to a lecture by an acknowledged scholar in whatever field you seek data. They will give you a context and they will give you facts to substantiate their findings and their understanding. If you want faith, read the Bible, the Koran, the Bhagavad-Gita or the Tao Te Ching and trust the context of their great source of truth. Use your brain. Relate it to what the world has learned. Put it into the context of the spirit in which it was written and you will have Truth (God) revealed to you and if you see (understand) you will be blessed. After all, the Son of God admonishes us to "hunger and thirst after righteousness." He said that the result would be a blessed state of being satisfied with what you consume.

So you see, my special, precious people, your grandpa has been a thinker for a long time and he hopes what follows will somehow encourage you to be thinkers, too. Don't just believe something because your mom or dad or I tell you to. Believe it because you have put it through the hard work and personal discipline of your own mind and experience. Listen to your mentors and elders but make up your own minds and create your own faith. Make it a personal thing that has its roots in God himself. Get to know him face-to-Face, heart-to-Heart, mind-to-Mind and spirit-to-Spirit.

Bill Cosby once did a comedy skit in which he took the part of Noah, conversing with God. As this funny routine concludes, Noah is exasperated and is really telling God how tough it has been to build the ark and fill it and all that goes with such an enormous project. He has had it and he tells God so. Finally, just when he is about to tell God to get somebody else to clean up the mess, he hears thunder in the distance and rain begins to fall. As the rain falls harder, Noah gets less and less intense until he whimpers what has become one of my favorite prayers and I hope it will become one of yours; he says in a very personal, prayerful way, "Okay, God . . . You and me!"

My precious grandchildren make it personal. Don't let it be religious. Create your own code of faith and behavior. Involve your God. Read the thoughts of those who have created their own codes. Take Jesus seriously. Get to know heroes of Christianity like Saint Francis or John Wesley. Become acquainted with the teachings of Buddha, Mohammad and other great people of all faiths. Sort them out. Develop your own code. That will make your life rich and you spirit strong and your relationship with your heavenly Father eternal.

What follows is a revised collection of some of the nearly 3,500 sermons I have written and preached over the last fifty years. They have been edited to fit the style of a book rather than a pulpit. They represent who I am and what God has helped me become. They have been written and rewritten with love and hope and faith. Take your time as you read them. The many repetitions are because they have become deeply ingrained in my mind and soul and are pertinent to the subject each one addresses. Read them with the full knowledge that I love God, I love you and I love myself. That's what the Bible calls "The Law and the Prophets." It is the essence of the Bible and the religion that has evolved from it.

As my friend Harry Fisher told me the night he assigned me to my first pastoral charge, "Bruce, be yourself." Be yourselves in the presence of your God who loves you and awaits your presence in heaven.

With all my love and affection,

Grandpa

ONE

Common Sense
Read: Psalm 119:105 and Matthew 6:25-34

Over the years, I have observed that a majority of American Christians build their religious faith on the thoughts of others. While these thoughts are important, it is also essential to create a personal base upon which to construct your faith. I think it is important for each person to discover how much of our personal spirituality comes from within and how much comes from significant authority figures in our lives. Ask yourself, "How much of what I believe is based on my personal thinking and my personal relationship with God, and how much of it is based on what others have told me I *should* believe?" What follows is an attempt to get you to be yourself. That's the best advice I ever got as I prepared for what has become a career as a preacher, teacher, pastor and chaplain, as well as a church administrator and innovator for pastoral ministry in parish and institutional settings. In Hamlet, Polonius advises his son Laertes: "To thine own self be true." It is as true today as it has always been. It makes good common sense within the context of the twenty-first century.

Around the time of the American Revolution, Thomas Payne wrote a popular pamphlet entitled "Common Sense." While I don't consider myself to be a revolutionary, I do believe common sense is one of the most important components in the exercise of theological self-definition. I have spent a lifetime searching the Bible and the writings of other people of faith, and I have found that common sense is also a common denominator. They are all profound because they don't attempt to overwhelm the reader. They speak to the common needs of everyone. Their goal is peace of mind and spirit and the eternal existence of the human soul.

I believe the Bible is the most common-sense book ever penned. Its characters, for the most part, are uncomplicated. That which they wrote (or was written about them) deals with everyday experiences not unfamiliar to people living today. I believe Christianity is a simple religion. I am disappointed that many of its adherents, both ancient and contemporary, are very prone to complicate it. If Jesus returned to this multi-denominational religion today, he might have difficulty recognizing the religion for which he is the foundation. From the beginning, fractures took place. Even Peter and Paul contributed, to some extent, to the excessive complexity that exemplifies the contemporary Church. I am saddened that the Church demands that everyone "do it our way or you'll rot in hell." Church affiliated institutions of higher education sometimes cloud the simple gospel with the intellectual snobbery of theological, philosophical, hermeneutical, historical and sociological sophistication. Don't get me wrong; without these disciplines, the Church would be governed and promulgated by ignorant cult leaders who give greater attention to emotion and tradition than they do to truth. There's enough of this already.

One of the main contributions of the intellectual community has been to safeguard the Church against rabble-rousers and shallow-thinking charismatics who prey on people's basic religious instincts and urge them to rely more on emotion than on rational thinking. The human being was created with a brain for a reason. Feeling without thought is shallow, transient, unstable, and too closely related to the time at hand. It is like a house that is built upon the sand. The storm of reality can undermine it and cause it to crumble and fall. In contrast, a life built upon the rock solid faith of people like Jesus' best known disciple, Peter, and common sense like the Holy Spirit that moved him, will stand the test of "labor and sorrow" (Psalm 90:10) and will survive and find peace, purpose and perspective.

The existence of modern Christianity and the Church can be explained with common sense. Think about it. The Bible isn't really that captivating a document. Large parts of it are boring and filled with information that does not catch the eye of the average seeker of wisdom and truth. There are some things that are not historically accurate. Conflicting dates are due to the fact that a common calendar didn't exist until long after the Bible had been compiled. Even its characters have conflicting names and relationships. Symbolic language can be misleading to the uninformed and those who are not willing to take the time to inform themselves. Too often readers do not take into consideration the evolution of language and realize that the meaning of some words has changed over the ages. Today, words like "fear," "terrible" and "awful" carry very negative connotations as opposed to their original meanings of respect, praise, and awe.

The Bible and the Church have been attacked by major world powers. Rational thinkers and highly respected intellectuals have seriously challenged its validity. Neither the Roman Empire nor the atheistic, totalitarian regimes of modern-day China and Russia have been able to extinguish the zeal of the Church Fathers. When Communism declined in the former Soviet Union and satellite countries, communities of faith and all that was necessary for them to exist appeared out of nowhere. Churches reopened. Bibles appeared. There was no lack of enthusiasm for worship. Why? It makes sense to me that there is a God who would not allow his way to be exterminated. He may allow it to be tested and attacked, but as the Bible says, "The gates of hell will not prevail against her." (Matthew 16:18) My personal belief is that the apathy and the heightened state of secular materialism in modern America will not defeat Christianity either. I have found that common-sense subjects make the greatest impact on congregations on Sunday morning or in prayer meetings and Bible studies during the week. Common sense speaks with much greater authority than a complicated, wordy exposition.

All I want out of life is to be at peace. I don't want to be confused by things I can't understand. I don't want to be overwhelmed by words and concepts that cloud the obvious and raise questions about that which I feel comfortable. However, I do recognize my need to be challenged. The role of adversity is acknowledged in that common-sense nugget of treasure buried deep in the Bible. In Psalm 90, the second half of verse 10, God says, "The strength of life is labor and sorrow." He is telling me to expect to have resistances thrown up at me, so I become strong enough to overcome them.

For example, when babies are born, they must overcome gravity in order to walk. They must conquer the resistance of parental "no's" to find a place in the family and the culture in which that family exists. Students need to study to overcome obstacles called examinations given by their teachers, who, prior to these traumatic episodes, have provided them with the necessary information to pass and succeed. If they overcome these obstacles, students can move on to greater challenges, but if they choose not to work and to take the road of least resistance, they will fail and (possibly) not grow intellectually. It is the same with the spiritual dimension of our lives. God allows bad things to happen to good people so they will become strong enough to grow into mature souls that he will welcome into heaven. While we may not like it, bodies, minds and spirits need resistance in order for growth to occur. Just as every top must have a bottom and every front a back, so there can be no happiness without the experience of sadness. There can be no success unless failure has been experienced. There can be no pleasure unless there is pain with which to compare it.

One of the reasons I am attracted to Jesus Christ is that he was a common-sense person. Yes, I believe him to be the Son of God. I accept with all my heart that "God was in Christ reconciling the world to himself." (II Corinthians 5:19) But I also find great comfort in how he expressed himself in the presence of people who were not of the religious elite. I am impressed by his behavior in the presence of those who thought they knew all the answers and who looked with disdain upon those who disagreed with them. Jesus was a common-sense person. He is the most outstanding personality of the Bible, even when compared to such Hebrew giants as Abraham, Jacob, Moses and David. They, too, were common-sense people. Their lives reflected straightforward, personal pronouncements of faith and behavior. Jesus' personal purity and consistently high level of personal integrity separate him from them. No man has ever displayed such a perfect and spotless character, free from that which seeks to impress others with intellect and rhetoric. He never assumed the human trait of self-aggrandizement. Jesus relied on simple parables and casual teaching methods to communicate the way and the truth. Jesus is the ultimate example of the fact that the Bible is a book of truth rather than a collection of facts.

Jesus is more appealing than David or Paul, whose complex minds expressed themselves in complicated writings and almost arrogant behavior. While each of these had his great moments of easily understandable, inspired expressions of faith, like Psalm 23, Romans or I Corinthians 13, for the most part they demanded to be respected for what they said more than for how they lived. The greatest insight from my study of these two men is the manner in which they overcame obvious personal deficiencies. David's self-serving conduct was manifest in adulterous behavior and being an accessory to murder because he tried to cover it up. His faith was evident, when—after being confronted by his personal conscience, Nathan—David repented sincerely and went on from there. This is much like what Jesus would have expected from the woman at the well. Her lifestyle was promiscuous but her hunger for God was genuine. Following her confession, Jesus said to her, "Go, and sin no more!" God communicated the same thing to David, and he, too, got on with his life.

Paul was a pharisaic zealot who was committed to exterminating the heretical followers of "The Way." (Jesus) He considered these crude and theological illiterates of the cult of the Nazarene carpenter to be an abomination and worthy of God's wrath. He did everything he could to eradicate them and their beliefs. But God spoke to Paul through the dying testimony of Stephen, the Christian deacon, whose execution Paul condoned. He heard God through Gamaliel, his honored mentor, who led him to rationally consider that if these people were of God, there was nothing he could do to stop the movement they espoused, and if they were not of God, they would spend their energy and the movement would go away in due time. Together these instruments of God's peace sparked the flames that would flash into a baptism by the Holy Spirit on the road to Damascus. The basic integrity and love for God that was in the heart of Saul of Tarsus would emerge and transform him from persecutor to believer. Like the Patriarch Jacob, who had been unethical in his dealings with his father and brother and who was willing to do anything to further his own agenda, so Saul would wrestle with God and would, like Jacob, be blessed.

The lives of both of these men were so altered that even their names changed. As Jacob, the supplanter, would become Israel, one who wrestles with God and is blessed, so Saul would become Paul, the missionary and chief architect of the Body we now know as the Church of Jesus Christ. Any person who is willing to allow the common sense of the conversion and transformation of these two giants of the Judeo-Christian tradition will also find that God is an understanding and gracious Lord, who consistently reaches out to anyone who is willing to be touched by him. I believe that a hysterical reaction that occurred in Paul's body initiated the blindness that inhibited him from completing his task of persecuting the small cell of followers of Jesus in Damascus. When Ananias took away the necessity of fulfilling his original plot, because he had now done a 180-degree turnabout theologically, socially and intellectually, he no longer needed to be blind. He didn't have to find these people, they found him and they loved him and he was saved, healed and consecrated to become a Christian of the highest order.

While scholars like Martin Luther rejected some biblical works such as the Epistle of James, I have found them to be significant and influential upon those to whom I have preached. People like James, Peter and Francis of Assisi appeal more to the general public than Augustine and Aquinas, who always seemed to lose me in their many words and complicated thoughts. Maybe I'm not disciplined enough or lack the intellectualism that marks Christians to whom these scholars appeal. I do know that I am a Commonsensible Contextualist. That's why I choose to put these thoughts onto paper.

When you read the book that is the focal point of the religion that bears the name of Jesus Christ, you will find a sensible path to guide you through life. If you seek first the Truth, (the Gospel of Jesus Christ) the details will become strangely insignificant. If you look for the commonsensible message of God through the people whose common denominator was faith in him and his humanness, I believe, like Thomas Payne, that such common sense will cause a revolutionary change in your life. It has in mine and it continues to do so every day.

TWO

Context, Context, Context

Read: Psalm 90:10, Isaiah 6:1-8, Malachi 3:1-6 and John 17:3

The Bible is greater than the legends that have been inspired by its characters, events and stories. It is more than the sum of its parts. It is truth more than it is fact. In his divine wisdom, Yahweh has seen fit to challenge the world with simplicity and common sense rather than complex religiosity. Conversely, it has been the work of the human mind and ego that has complicated his revelation. The church's greatest sin has been to obscure the simple common-sense message of God by confusing the context in which it has been revealed with speculation, provincialism and intellectualizing. Too often she has made herself the end rather than a means to the end for which she was established—to make the Word of God come alive in us.

The divine challenge is evident in that the truth, which God wants us all to embrace, is so plainly communicated. But we, who are endowed with brains that have been designed to compute complicated mathematical calculations and discover the nature and the structure of things from the atom to the universe, from animal organisms to the human psyche, from the rocks in the earth to the composition of celestial bodies, seem to be inclined to see the forest rather than the trees. In other words, God's truth is, has been, and always will be right before our eyes, in a context that can only be described as commonsensible, but we seem to want to make it more complex than it really is. For some reason, we seem to believe that divinity is sophisticated and simplicity is not holy. If it is of God, we say, it must demand our most refined mental gymnastics. After all, how can such a wondrous message be so simple?

Moses expressed the very foundation of my personal faith and spiritual life. Tradition testifies that his words are buried near the middle of the Bible, (Psalm 90) like precious gems or valuable natural resources. God inspired him to say that life's strength and quality can only be understood through hard work and overcoming the many obstacles we encounter as we grow and mature. We grow, become stronger and achieve divine approval only when we overcome the ordinary, divinely programmed challenges and obstructions that are designed to build human achievements. A baby grows by expanding his lungs with screams of protest in the frustration of not getting what he wants. The infant matures when she overcomes gravity and graduates from crawling to toddling, then walking and running and climbing. Each phase of our maturation comes in due time, when we have done the work that has been planned by the divine mind of our Creator. Truly the wisdom of the words: "The strength of life is labor and sorrow" (Psalm 90:10) is manifest within the context of human life.

Context is like a catalyst in a chemical reaction. It causes the reaction but doesn't necessarily enter into its final composition. Human maturity occurs only when resistances confront the person, who can only overcome them by working and submitting himself to the discipline of learning and faith. Failure is not a deterrent for the maturing human being, it is the context which needs to be overcome and defeated in order for the person to move on to greater abilities and accomplishments. Only through this context will the strength be developed that enables one to take the next step in a progression of steps that lead to eventual success.

I contend that it is the context of life that enables one to understand what makes these reactions take place. Only in the context of time and faith in the plan of God, as outlined in Holy Scripture, can a person accomplish anything. A willingness to discipline oneself by paying the price of hard work and expending the physical, mental and spiritual energy needed to move forward can one prepare for the next challenge. Until the day the human breathes his or her last, there will always be another day and another challenge. As the prophet Malachi foretold, the spirit of God will be like a refiner's fire. (Malachi 3:3)

He will purify us like a refiner purges impurities from gold and silver that we may become righteous, holy and acceptable in his sight; that we might be worthy of hearing from him those coveted words, "Well done, good and faithful servant." (Matthew 25:23)

In Psalm 90:10, the inspired writer used the word "sorrow." As anyone who takes physical fitness seriously knows, there is no gain without pain. And there is no light without the dispelling of darkness and no life unless labor pains are endured. There is no worth or quality unless impurities have been purged by fire and pressure. There is no salvation without repentance. There is no redemption without the blood of the Lamb being shed.

Jacob was reformed when he wrestled with God. Saul became Paul, the great Apostle, only after he fought the battle within his conscience and overcame his blindness to the truth. Your sinful life and mine cannot be redeemed unless we are born again following God's labor of love and our deliverance by faith. Unless we allow the Holy Spirit to purge our sin, we will remain alienated and estranged from God. Whether you like it or not, the only way to a holy union with your God is to endure the labor and sorrow of repentance and discipline within the context of faith as it exists in your personal life. Reading the Bible or going to church won't do it. Being religious is not enough. "You must be born again," (John 3:7) remains a major premise upon which the classic Christian proclamation of faith, hard work, self-discipline and personal repentance is built.

The context of all of this is what reveals the truth. The vehicle for it is the Bible and its stories of human frailty and struggle. Jesus said that eternal life comes to those who know God intimately (John 17:3), and such intimacy has a price. It is not so much the cost of expending one's intellect as much as it is the product of the passion of the soul. Only then is a new life conceived and the eternal person enabled to be born again.

Story after story and passage after passage of biblical literature illustrate this truth. It becomes realized within the mind of a believer surrounded by the context of his or her life. When a person intellectualizes who said what, when it was said, to whom it was said, where it was said, under what conditions it was said and during what historical time it was said, the context of Holy Writ can be established. It is between the lines or behind the scenes of a Bible story or character that the truth of the story is revealed. It is the unwritten truth that is exposed *after* the story has been told and the truth realized in the refinery of hard work and personal overcoming of life's obstacles that salvation occurs.

The way and the truth that Jesus claimed to be can only be revealed in the context of your life, when you are introduced to him by the Bible and become acquainted with his life, message and ministry. Like Saint Paul, you need to walk the path of intellectual conflict, wrestle with the principalities of humanism, the spiritual Adversary and your own ego. Then you will be healed of the blindness that comes from being exposed to the bright light of one's personal conviction of sin. When the Apostle wrestled with the faith of Stephen, the wisdom of his mentor, Gamaliel, and the intervention of the Holy Spirit, he found the common sense of the Gospel within the context of personal turmoil. It was then that he was born again and grew to become the one many believe to be the most influential person of the New Testament, aside from Jesus.

A grandfather's responsibility is sometimes hidden because he is supposed to fade into the background and enjoy retirement. However, it is also his responsibility to challenge the two generations that follow him to grow up. One way to do this is to take a risk and challenge that which his children and grandchildren have assumed.

In this regard, let me urge you to think that just maybe the spirit you know as Satan (also known as the Devil or the Adversary) is not what tradition and spiritual lore has made him to be. For a long time I have been wrestling with the thought that maybe Satan isn't God's enemy, sworn to destroy the Lord of the universe, but to be his faithful servant, a duly ordained *loyal opposition*, as it were. Like a personal trainer urging more and more resistance that strengthens the body, so just *maybe* Satan's role is to be that resistance, that spiritual opposition designed to strengthen your soul and fulfill Psalm 90:10's truth that the "strength of life *is* labor and sorrow."

Let me cite two well-known events from the Bible. In the Old Testament the story of Job begins with God and Satan having a discussion about a righteous man named Job. God contends that Job is an unwavering saint and Satan believes he can be tempted to turn against God. Their confrontation is well-known. Through it all, Job wrestles with his God and the unfairness of life but never curses God or forsakes his faith. He is angry and acts like any unfairly treated human would act. In the end, he is vindicated because he knows that his Redeemer lives and he believes that God will justify and sanctify him. (Job 19:25f) That's what happened. Satan did his job. Job was faithful. God blessed him in the end.

Another incident is recorded in the New Testament. Jesus, is led by the Holy Spirit into the wilderness to be tested by the Devil. (Matthew 4) Why? Well, that's how he became strong enough to do what he had to do to influence the people of the world to know God. Was Satan God's enemy or his instrument of spiritual strength and growth? I don't know, but it has been an interesting few years in which I have pondered this question.

My point is this. It is not the facts my question raises that interests me. It is the truth that I discover about myself and my relationship with my Abba who wants me to be strong and faithful and ready to will his will and to know him. He isn't afraid he will lose me but he doesn't want me to lose myself.

I challenge you to think about it and wrestle with it. Remember that the name Israel means "He who wrestles with God." (Genesis 32:28) God is a god of grace and your faith is the key to it. It comes by wrestling with that which is unknown and beyond human understanding. If God is to bless you, you must be willing to be a blessing to him and overcome the sparring of Satan in order to achieve this holy and lofty goal. I believe that is the lesson of the last Beatitude (Matthew 5:10, 11). Those of us who trust God and are willing to be vulnerable, for his sake will take up our crosses and follow the example of Jesus. We will overcome the temptation to run from that which would separate us from God and face it head on with faith. Then, by his grace, we will achieve the gift of eternal life.

Context dwarfs the words of the Bible and the people who wrote or spoke them. I find that common sense, when mixed with the context of the people, events and the teachings of the Bible, produces Truth with a capital "T." Biblical facts, statements and stories need to be given value within another context—the existential moment, the present. In other words, the time, personalities, and events of the Bible need to be mixed with similar entities of the present, create a context of truth more than a collection of facts. Put all of what I have said together and mix thoroughly in the mind and the soul of a sinner like me and a new insight can be born. I have wrestled for a lifetime and have decided to call what I believe Commonsensible Contextualism. It fits me better than terms like liberal or conservative, orthodox or Gnostic, Protestant or Catholic, Presbyterian or Methodist, Christian, Jew, Muslim, Buddhist or any other religious label.

All God's children have one Father and he could care less about the labels we wear religiously, nationally, intellectually, philosophically, politically or socially. What does matter is the context in which a person comes to know God and share that intimate knowledge with one's fellow human beings. In that great day the believer will find the truth of the Great Commandment that asserts that, no matter what our faith or religion, we should love the Lord God with all of our heart, mind, soul and strength and that we should profess that same love to the rest of those who share this planet with us, as well as with ourselves. (Luke 10:25-28) At that moment in time, I believe, the covenant between God and Abraham is finally realized. The believer will be blessed because he or she will have truly become a blessing. (Examine Genesis 12:2.)

THREE

Questions, Questions, Questions

Whether it's writing a sermon or an article for a newspaper, a magazine, a journal or a book, one has to always answer the "big six" questions. They are: who, what, why, how, when and where? As we cross the landscape of Commonsensible Contextualism, it is important that we address these basic queries. In them a framework is created upon which is built a thoughtful structure of one's personal life within a context of common-sense faith and religion; one that helps one mature and move beyond elementary religion.

I believe the "who" of Commonsensible Contextualism is extremely important. Obviously when one establishes a religious point of view, the most important subject is God and the most significant question to be asked is "Who is he?" My search for spiritual truth leads me to conclude that God has revealed himself in many ways to every age and culture and that he has revealed himself to me within the context of common sense. I needed a place to begin, so, since I am a Christian, I decided to begin there. I can truly say that this approach has put me on shaky ground in the eyes of many who share with me Jesus Christ as Lord and Savior. Our differences seem to focus on whether we *literally* accept the words on the pages of the Bible or interpret them contextually.

Take one of the foundational statements of the John's Gospel, for example: "God so loved the *world* that He gave His only begotten Son, that *whoever* believes in him shall not perish but have everlasting life." (John 3:16) The terms "world" and "whoever" broaden the context, thereby creating a conflict. It says that the world is the stage upon which God reveals himself, then it narrows the field to those "whoever" believe in *him*.

Does it mean that you *must* accept Jesus as the divinely incarnate Son of God in order to be saved from your sin and ensured eternal life in heaven, or can you find that acceptance some other way within the context of *your* world culture, family, religion, etc.? Don't forget, the Bible says, "In the beginning, God created the heavens and the earth." (Genesis 1:1) That widens the context tremendously. Such talk on my part has tended to threaten more provincially thinking Christians. They see God only from the image *they* have created or the one *they* have accepted that has been created for *them*. Could it be that if God created the universe, he cannot be restricted to being present within provincialisms such as "western-thinking Americans" or "middle eastern-thinking Muslims" or "far eastern-thinking Buddhists"? There's got to be some common sense here. God is not only holy, he is catholic (universal) in the strictest sense and if he is universal, every creature within that ultimate context has a right to respond to him as he reveals himself personally and individually to them.

For years I have wrestled with John 14:6, which says, "I am the Way, the Truth and the Life, *no one* comes to the Father but by *Me*." This challenges me to restrict the inhabitants of heaven to only those who choose the Gospel of Jesus Christ. But then the Holy Spirit confronts me with the words of Jesus in another scriptural setting, Luke 10:25ff. It is that time when Jesus enlightened a Pharisaic Jew with Mosaic thinking. He used the enduring words of the Shema (Hear, O Israel), the seminal words of the Torah (the Law). He said, "If you love God with your heart, mind, soul and strength and love your fellow human beings as much as you love yourself, you will live (go to heaven)." As hard as I might try, I can't escape the penetrating words of Psalm 90:10, which say that the strength of a person's life is his or her labor and sorrow (hard work and personal discipline). No two passages of scripture have caused me more concern and demanded more of my personal discipline than these two, because I know that when I honestly wrestle with God and am willing to do so within the context of my life, he will bless me as he blessed Jacob, who wasn't afraid to confront God until he was blessed.

So I press on. Somehow, someway, somewhere within the context of those two statements, God has opened his Kingdom to the *whole* of his creation. So, who is God? The Jews call him Yahweh, "I AM." That works for me. *God is!* It is simple and understandable and free from manipulation into some complicated interpretation. "God is!" Like the bumper sticker says: "The Bible says it. I believe it. That settles it."

Islam says that God is "THE God." (Allah) This appears to be in harmony with what Jews and Christians believe. The Ten Commandments state emphatically, "Thou shalt have no *other* gods before Me." In other words, "You will hold no other gods (power, prestige, money, possessions, self, etc.) in greater esteem than Me." (Yahweh).

So, why all the trouble between these people? For fifteen hundred years they have been calling each other names, killing each other and denigrating each other's religion. The Bible and the Koran testify to the reconciliation between Jacob and his twin brother Esau. Why can't their descendants do the same? Because they have their context mixed up. They are self-centered provincial religionists who can't stand sharing the love of the God Christians call Abba. As Jacob and Esau shared the same father, why can't those who acknowledge Allah-Yahweh-Abba as their commonly hallowed God?

Now, if you think we Christians are free from criticism, let me remind you that we too have put God into our own provincial, denominational, philosophical and religious box. There are times when we don't even try to make sense out of the phrase, "God so loved the *world*." We become so wrapped up in our own religion that we can't or won't even consider the possibility that God just might have revealed himself to other people in other ways and through other prophets. "Who is God?" is a question that has prompted such narrow and strident thinking that wars have been waged, martyrs have been created, families have been destroyed, friendships have been lost and clear-thinking minds have been clouded.

In AD 1099, for example, followers of Jesus, whom they affirmed to be the Prince of Peace, slaughtered, in his name, more than 40,000 people in Jerusalem in just one day because they were judged to be "infidels." It was a "holy crusade" sponsored by the Church to return that city to the hands of its "rightful" owners. No wonder Muslims are angry with us. This is not even to mention the anti-Semitic violence that has been prevalent in Europe for hundreds of years and which was seen during the reign of terror brought about by Hitler and his Nazi Party.

God said it best when he told Moses, "I AM who I AM!" Why not let it go at that? The Lord says in Revelation 3:20, "Behold, I stand at the door and knock. If anyone hears [understands] my voice [word] and opens the door [trusts], I will come in and eat with him and he with me." Do you hear what God is saying? "Here I am. If you truly want me, I'll come to you and we will have fellowship (get to "know" each other) and I will nourish you." He will come to anyone, any time, anywhere, but first you have to really listen to him, not to tradition, custom or myth.

What does your heart hear from God? Listen. He is there and he is communicating and he is making sense. In the context of my life, I have grown to know him and trust him, not because he is the God of the Presbyterian Christians but because he is *the* God, *my* heavenly Father. His name says it all: Yahweh Allah Abba.

The second question is "what?" Go back and read what I said about "who" God is. I will acknowledge that there are descriptive terms that expand on the name of God and help answer the "what?" Things like infinite (Ein Sof), omniscient, omnipotent, omnipresent, etc.; descriptive titles like Creator, Redeemer, Friend, Counselor, Advocate, Way, Truth and Life. A paradox exists here. His simplicity is evident. But when you seek to analyze him, it becomes impossible to plumb the depths of his being. No wonder God is the object of so many religions. They have all been created within the minds of human beings to make sense out of that which they cannot comprehend. And, all too many times, they have created him in *their* image rather than accepting the image in which he created them.

Why is God? In 1 Corinthians 15, Saint Paul gives a great answer. He said, in so many words, "Because I AM said so." The Apostle used the example of a seed that is planted and grows into a body "as God has chosen." There is no other answer. What happens happens because the Creator of it all says it will. It's like God saying, "I Am who I AM . . . *because I said so.*" God is because he chose to be. Things are because God thought of them. Genesis 1 says, "And God said, 'Let there be light.' And it was so." Once again, faith provokes me to exclaim, "God said it. I believe it. That settles it!"

How is God? There's an old joke that asks how you will react if confronted by a two-ton gorilla. The answer is: any way he wants. He is in charge. He rules. If you don't like it, stop the world and get off. You can doubt God, argue with him and even ignore him. Thomas and Job tried to doubt and argue with him and he blessed both of them. They came to the same conclusion after they had honestly "wrestled" with God." They professed from the depths of their souls: "My Lord and my God!"

Where and when is God? The answer is simply, here and now. God has been here and now ever since the "here and now" began. Religion has been trying to make sense out of this since religions began. Those based on rational common sense have gotten the right answer and used it for a foundation of faith. In my estimation the religion designed by Paul and Peter and their spiritual descendents, built on Jesus Christ, did it best.

What I have said might raise some questions in your mind as to its value. I think that is good. Honest doubt is the foundation upon which viable faith is built. Honest searching for truth isn't easy. What you have just read are some conclusions I have come to over the years. I am confident when I say that I too am who I am and this is what I am becoming. I believe it all stands or falls on what I believe I have inherited from THE God (Allah) my Father (Abba) who IS (Yahweh) without end (Ein Sof). And he will always be. He is in me and I am his image yearning to be true.

FOUR

Independence and Individuality
Read: Matthew 16:24-28 and II Chronicles 7:11-19

In America, July 4th is called Independence Day. It is a time to recall how America chose to stand alone and be accountable for her own destiny. We get a lot of satisfaction each time we realize the significance of our country's contribution to the maturing of the human race. We honor those who paid the ultimate price to achieve and maintain this liberty and we bestow high honors on those who willingly sacrificed much to keep it for us, our children and hopefully for our children's children.

Thomas Jefferson wrote that we were a new nation conceived in liberty. He quickly learned that this new country would not be born unless her people were willing to endure the labor that would naturally deliver her. This venerable patriot acknowledged, as so many other wise men and women have since, that God's universal principle of growth and strength (Psalm 90:10) must always be fulfilled in order to attain such high and lofty goals. A productive life will grow and gain strength only when the person or the society is willing to work and sacrifice for the benefits that come with independent self-realization.

The United States and the Church of Jesus Christ share a similarity. Both have come into being and remain vibrant and influential because individuals have been willing to lay down their lives for the many to live in freedom and to be able to manifest their personal and corporate destinies. These two historically significant bodies have affirmed what the Bible has revealed. In order for a person or a nation to be born, he, she or it must have faith in the sacrificial blood of those called by God to lay down their lives to cover the cost of salvation and/or freedom.

As the blood of the ancient Paschal Lamb was shed to cause the angel of death to pass over the homes of believers, so the blood of thousands of American lambs has frustrated those who would kill our sacred liberty. As personal salvation comes to those who are born again, so too will this nation, born in 1776, be born again when her people call on the name of God and humble themselves and pray. Then he will hear them and heal their land and honor their faith. (II Chronicles 7:14) Only then will God bless America, *if* . . .

God's covenant with Abraham (Genesis 12:2) was a simple contract between two consenting individuals. God promised to bless the Patriarch *if* and *when* he would fulfill his part of the agreement, and that was to be a blessing in return. It was no different than any contract between an employer and an employee: you work for me and I will pay you. In this case, I will bless you if you bless me. This is nothing more than a straight forward treaty within the context of God and his faithful servant, Abraham, the father of the Jews, the Christians and the Muslims. I don't think it is far-fetched to believe that such a contract is available to America. We sing and pray "God bless America." But for that to be fulfilled, America must bless God in return.

Salvation comes when a person is born again. It is made possible because God became an individual and by his great grace gave his life so the believer could have freedom to choose to be saved. Salvation is *not* a corporate act. It is a covenant of grace between God and an individual. However, it can occur within the context of a corporate body such as a nation or a religion whose collective membership desires it so much that they together trust God and sacrifice their lives after the manner of their Savior and national Patron. While one's religion or nationality might help, it all boils down to the personal relationship the individual *chooses* to accept within the plan of God's divine grace and his supreme understanding of the human condition.

Jesus plainly articulated his formula for personal independence to those he chose to be his disciples. Like so many who helped build America, the people Jesus chose were those of common stature but uncommon in their faith and courage. He let them know, in no uncertain terms, that their lives could very well be required should they choose to follow him. He made it absolutely clear that he expected them to be willing to give much before they would get what they coveted most—freedom from the bondage of sin and worldly domination. Here again, the Bible testifies to the fact that there is no gain without the pain and the sorrow of personal discipline.

It is important that you take time and make an effort to listen to what Jesus said to the Twelve and to do so within the context of that time, place and company. You should guard against allowing tradition and immature faith and logic to dilute the passion necessary to fulfill his call to arms. Don't permit humanistic rationalism to weaken the power of his words. Hear what the Lord Jesus Christ, required of those who became forefathers of your Christian faith, those who fought for your spiritual independence. Pay attention to his words recorded in Matthew 16: 24-26.

Allow me to amplify his thoughts. I do so only after much prayer and contemplation. Jesus said, "If anyone would come after me [join me, follow me] let him [her] deny himself and take up a cross." I don't think anyone could have asked for a more graphic symbol of personal devotion and sacrifice than to project a possible crucifixion as a result of choosing to be a part of a band of believers that attended to Jesus.

He went on to say, "Whosoever would save his life [soul] will lose it; and whosoever will lose his life, for my sake, will find it." In other words, if you are more concerned with saving your physical, material, economic and social life, you will lose the opportunity to achieve eternal life, but if you want to abide forever in the presence of God, then you need to be willing to, by faith, lay down your life in obedience to him.

Clearly, Jesus is proclaiming that freedom, salvation and redemption will only come to those who are sincerely willing to sacrifice their lives and discipline their minds for his sake and in his name; those who will hunger and thirst after righteousness; those who are willing to become poor in spirit, meek, and able to endure being vulnerable for others; those who are willing to be merciful peacemakers (Matthew 5:3-10); those who are justified by faith (Romans 1:17); and those who are saved by his grace (Romans 3:23-24). In short, those who wish to win eternal freedom will be those who are willing to let the word of God come alive within the depths of their hearts, minds and souls and dare to put their bodies on the line too.

Matthew 16:26 makes sense out of these apparently unreasonable demands. Jesus theorizes, "What will it profit a person if he gains the whole physical world and forfeits his soul?" Could it be that our Lord was reminded of the experience he had had in the wilderness and the beginning of his ministry when Satan so vigorously tempted him? Was he recalling that Satan, his "spiritual trainer," had offered him instant worldly power, influence, and fame if he would abandon his divine mission of redemption?

Right from the start, Jesus wanted to know if his lieutenants would be up to paying the price for their commission in the army of his Father's kingdom. He knew at first hand the cost of the temporal sorrow and personal discipline they would be required to expend. Were they up to it? I think certainly so. Was this an outrageous demand? How would you feel if it was made of you?

Most every American president has asked for similar responses from the citizens of our great country. Patriots of the Revolution were asked. Sons of the North and sons of the South were asked. Sons and daughters of America were asked in 1941, 1951, 1961, 1991, 2001 and 2011. Their blood was spilled on Iwo Jima and in Korea, Viet Nam, Kuwait, Afghanistan and Iraq. Come to think of it, Jesus didn't ask of Peter, Andrew and John and the rest anything much different than most of the presidents of the United States have asked of their people.

Lay down your life for that which is bigger than you or greater than you and you will reap the rewards of a grateful God or an appreciative nation. John Kennedy is remembered for having asked of us what Jesus similarly asked twenty-one centuries before. Kennedy said, "Ask not what your country can do for you; rather ask what you can do for your country." Like Kennedy, other presidents haven't hesitated to call for sacrifice, and neither did Jesus the Christ. We know of Kennedy's willingness to lay down his own life for the crew of his navy boat, the PT 109. We are also aware that Jesus was willing to pay the same price he was asking his disciples to consider. Our God never hesitates to *do* what he asks of those who choose to follow him. Christ is believable and worthy of our loyalty because he put his life on the same line he asked his disciples to accept. He did it graphically when he fought the Battle of Calvary Hill. He lived it. I believe it. If he asks me, I will do it, too.

Independence Day will come and go. So let me ask: Are you willing to fight for your individual soul or for the life of America or the existence of the church or for the safety of you family under the same conditions Jesus demanded of his disciples? Only you can answer this question. Unless each of us does our individual best, the rest of us will collectively fail.

The Church is the same. She depends on the collective and corporate strength of individual believers beginning with Peter and the disciples and the forbearers of every denomination to the founders of every local congregation. Unless each individual does his or her part the Church will die or, at least, suffer the fate of Israel and be taken captive for a time of discipline and reformation.

In the spirit of the wisdom of Solomon found in Ecclesiastes 3, let me reiterate that there is a time for everything under the sun. There is a time for individualism and a time for corporate togetherness. There is a time for you and a time for your country. There is a time for you and a time for me, as well as a time for God and a time for you and me. There is a time to lead and a time to follow; a time to be alone and a time to join the Body of Christ; and there is a time to be born again and a time to die for your God.

When the time is ripe you will know it. If you are sensitive to his Holy Spirit, God will show you the way. There is still room for a spirit of individuality and a spirit of independence, but there is also a time when all of this will have its greatest meaning—the time when it is gathered under the banner of Christ and we are brought together with disciples of all ages, all denominations, all perspectives, contexts, races, nations and personalities that coexist within the bounds of his eternal heavenly Kingdom.

FIVE

Face to Face with God

Read: Psalm 8 and Genesis 25-32

In the course of my lifetime, I have been attracted to the personal nature of the King of the universe. I find it difficult to comprehend this wondrous fact. It is beyond my capacity to understand how the Creator, Sustainer and Redeemer of the world could possibly be aware of me. Like David, I can exclaim, "When I consider the work of your hands, the moon and the stars, which you have established, who am I that you are mindful of me?" (Psalm 8:3,4)

A long time ago, I determined that Jesus Christ is and always will be my personal Savior. I have accepted this the same way I accept the beating of my heart or the process of breathing. It is second nature for me and easily taken for granted. I can honestly say that when I close my eyes and bow my head I expect God to be there, ready, willing and able to care enough to listen to my plea or hear my cry or enjoy my unique praise. But maturity brings an erosion of youthful innocence and blind childlike faith. Growing up means facing reality and investigating the cause and effect of things that confront us in life. The older we get, the more we seek logical answers to the "big six" questions we touched upon earlier. Faith is tested by skepticism and reason and innocent idealism dissolve into sophisticated rationalism.

But God is good. He loves and understands us. He walked the walk of human experience. He consciously chose to live as one of us in order to reveal his universal truth to anyone who would take the time and make the effort to search for it and to work and be disciplined enough to overcome the natural obstacles that lie in the way. He revealed this truth through disciples like John, the Apostle, who many believe wrote in the Book of Revelation, "Behold, I stand at the door [of your mind and spirit] and knock; if you hear my voice and open the door I will come in and eat with you." (Revelation 3:20)

One of my favorite rational Bible stories conveys this truth. It's about Jacob, the son of Isaac, the grandson of Abraham, father of the twelve tribes of Israel. It's about how he stood toe-to-toe with God and didn't flinch. There isn't a more immature or childish personality in the Bible than Jacob. He played nasty juvenile tricks on his brother, Esau, by taking advantage of his shallow personality and lustful human nature. He also deceived his father in order to promote his own personal agenda.

Esau had been hunting and came home famished. Foolishly he allowed Jacob to swindle his birthright in exchange for a bowl of cereal. This meant that he allowed his brother to replace him in the order of inheritance of Isaac's considerable wealth. All Jacob could think of, at that moment, was enhancing his future. All Esau could think of, at that moment, was satisfying his physical hunger. Sound familiar? When you were a kid, didn't you focus more on satisfying the moment rather than planning ahead and ensuring your future?

To add to the list of self-centered childish behavior, the younger brother would later stick it to his older brother again by deceiving their aged father into bestowing a coveted paternal blessing on Jacob under false pretenses. It happened when Jacob, his mother's favorite, masqueraded as Esau, who, incidentally, was his father's favorite.

Isaac was old and feeble and unable to see or hear very well, so Jacob dressed in animal skins and prepared deer meat stew like Esau often did for his father, and lied about who he was. Because of the stew and the "hairy body" Isaac believed him. It was a piece of cake to deceive the old man and, as a result, the irreversible paternal blessing was bestowed on the wrong son. For some reason I can't understand, this could not be reversed when the truth was discovered. Be that as it may, it happened, and Jacob fled from the understandable wrath of his embittered brother.

Years passed, and both boys grew to be men and accumulated considerable families and material wealth of their own. Isaac still lived and I guess Jacob's conscience began to bother him. He had matured and had felt the pain of deceit himself by his father-in-law, Laban. It made him grow up and realize the errors of his ways with respect to his brother. So he sent a representative to Esau and arranged a meeting to reconcile with him. To appease his brother, he smothered him with gifts and removed his wives and children from harm's way. He hoped for the best but prepared for the worst Esau could possibly heap upon him.

The primary lesson of this story comes during the night before the estranged brothers are to finally meet and reconcile. In the wee hours of the morning, while Jacob fretted about what would happen when the two met, a strange and life-altering thing happened. During those lonely hours of anticipation, when emotions are always more sensitive, there appeared to Jacob a "person" with whom he wrestled. Was it a dream? Was the person real or imagined? Was it God or an angel? What are the details? Is it really important, or is the result of the change that came upon our troubled hero the only thing that can really count? The truth of the matter is what counts. It is what *always* counts. The truth is more important than the facts. No matter how it happened, Jacob's life was forever changed because in his heart, mind and soul he had faced God and stood strong and resolute in his faith.

As morning approached, the person commanded Jacob to release him, but he refused. Jacob realized that he had come to grips with God and vowed he would not let go until the Lord blessed him for his efforts and repentance. So intense was Jacob's determination and so deep were his convictions that the only thing that would break his hold was physical pain. Jacob's thigh was dislocated, and God came to realize the repentant patriarch's spiritual pain; and by his grace and through his divine understanding of this wayward son, God fulfilled the prayer and blessed him.

The physical pain was evidently not as bad as the emotional and spiritual pain of Jacob's guilt. The sincerity and depth of his repentance touched the Lord so much that he blessed Jacob, relieved his fear and strengthened his spirit. Now he could face his brother and accept whatever would happen, knowing that he had been restored to his heavenly Father's good graces. To top off this magnificent moment, God told the patriarch that from henceforth his name would no longer be Jacob (the supplanter, meaning the displacer or the one who dislodges) but Israel, which means "he who wrestles with God." Truly the wayward son of Isaac and the deceptive brother of Esau had wrestled with a higher power (as well as with himself) and was changed. Jacob's faith had built a maturity that gave him the courage to face God, himself and his brother. Together the brothers went to be with their father in his dying days. I'm sure this brought much joy and peace to the heart and mind of Isaac.

There are several other Bible stories whose context reveals much the same lesson as the story of Jacob/Israel. Job faced God in sorrow and in grief and was restored. David sought the face of the Lord. He received grace and mercy that was greater than his sin. Peter's fear was removed when he stood before his resurrected Christ and confessed his failure as a friend. Paul was healed of the blindness that had hidden that knowledge which eventually would lead him to enlighten the whole world and account for innumerable souls redeemed by the grace of God, the love of Christ and the power of the Holy Spirit. Even the nameless woman at the well stood above her checkered past as she looked into the eyes of Christ and felt his compassionate understanding.

You need to *know* that it is *not* a sin to disagree or even argue with God; nor is it wrong to doubt. From such experiences can come deeper meaning and greater purpose in one's relationship with God. It can be the breeding ground for a closer relationship. It can fulfill Richard of Chitester's threefold prayer: " . . . to see Thee more clearly, love Thee more dearly and follow Thee more nearly, day by day"; to understand, to know and love intimately and to serve. If you can face such an experience with faith and with full knowledge that God's grace is sufficiently greater than human nature and behavior, you will come to know a great and divine truth.

The independent thinker has no individuality until he or she steps out from behind the wall of immaturity, tradition and superstition and faces God. Only then does one experience the depth of honest thought, feeling and faith. Such common sense can be discovered within the context of biblical stories such as the ones I have mentioned and many more that I did not. Take the story of Thomas, the "doubter," for instance. I believe he just might be the most truthful of the disciples. He needed to discover for himself what his friends had claimed, that Jesus had risen from the dead. Because of it he has suffered the role of being the scapegoat for all who would search his mind and soul and want more than merely what others have said. Peter and John didn't believe at first and we don't label them doubters. Remember, like Jacob, Thomas came to his own acceptance and in his own way found that for which his greatest dreams were realized. When Jesus came to him and revealed himself, the Apostle fell to his knees and confessed, "My Lord and my God!"

These stories are great, but unless you put them into the context of your own life, they are merely cherished gems of religious lore. When they become objects of faith within the unique personal context of your relationship with God, they will reveal their true value and you, like Jacob, David, Peter, Thomas, Paul and millions of other honest, forthright souls, will be blessed and enter into that special personal and open relationship with your God.

SIX

Think Three

Read: Genesis 12:1-3; 17; Matthew 28:19, 20;
Acts 16:25-34 and I Corinthians 13:13

Commonsensible Contextualism is as simple as one, two, three. One need not be a rocket scientist or have a photographic memory to adequately struggle with comprehending the mysteries of God's revelation of himself. An ability to use one's natural mental resources within the context of common human sense and religious faith is all that is needed. On the other hand, advanced education has and does contribute greatly; for example, the work of linguistic scholars, archeologists, anthropologists, sociologists, philosophers, historians and theologians.

There should be no excuse for you not to know all there is to know about God. Conversely, these great contributors cannot be a substitute for your coming to know God (John 17:3) intimately through personal faith, common sense and openness to the context of his revelation through his Word, his Church and his Holy Spirit.

Religion has a problem: its people and institutions have taken themselves too seriously. The Church, with all her greatness, has too often fallen prey to an elevated opinion of herself. She may be the Body of Christ, but only a personal, intimate relationship with him will ensure eternal salvation. It is faith in Christ that saves not membership in the Church. He has revealed the image of God much more than religion has. The Church has complicated the common sense of the spiritual context as proclaimed through God's incarnate Son. She has too often been concerned with *her* image rather than his will. This has been a difficult reality for me to accept because I love the Church. She has been a major reason for my relationship with God. She has contributed immensely to my knowledge, both intimate and cerebral, of him.

However, since coming to know him, I have had to modify much of what the Church has taught me. Too often she has been responsible for the image of God that the world has come to accept. He is *not* the image the Church has created. The truth is, *we* have been created in *his* image and that defies the many traditional images that have evolved over the last twenty-one centuries.

Saint Paul was a scholar. His ability to articulate that which he believed is exceptional. He had the ability to enhance his considerable exposure to the best education his family's resources and the times could afford. All this has given him great credibility over the centuries since he drew up the religious architectural specifications for what has become the Christian Church. Scholars and theologians have trusted his insights. The writings of the Apostle to the Gentiles are incorporated in the New Testament. They are the primary instruments by which the theological superstructure of the Church was constructed. But keep in mind, the foundation upon which all of this is anchored is Jesus Christ and the Gospels that have been inspired to proclaim his message.

The writings of Paul are more than those of any other contributor to the New Testament. Scholars argue over which ones he wrote and which ones were written in his name by anonymous writers (Ephesians, Hebrews, Timothy, and Titus). I respect and believe most of what is contained in these epistles but I cannot equate them with the words of Jesus Christ. Common sense has led me to divide the Bible into three divisions rather than two. I call them the Hebrew Testament, the Gospel and the Apostolic Testament. I do not, in any way, want you to think I have no respect for men like Paul, Peter, John or James. But I just cannot equate them with Jesus Christ. It seems to me that these great men are not as authoritative as the Lord Jesus. I also think that there have been many, many other similarly inspired writers whose works have not been incorporated into the Bible. I have been inspired by ancients like Augustine, Aquinas, and even some of the Gnostics. Contemporaries like Karen Armstrong, Billy Graham, Elaine Pagels, and many others whose works I have read and loved have drawn me closer to my God and motivated me to turn inward and trust my own insights.

I appreciate the way Saint Paul received God's revelation through the Holy Spirit and explicated his own personal relationship with Jesus. I too have been caught between divine revelation and the opinions of the establishment. I too have composed hundreds of sermons, and I too believe that God's Holy Spirit was as much my inspiration as he was to all the superstars mentioned above. I think it is only common sense to believe that many present-day writers have earned equal respect with those of the apostolic age. God did not cease to inspire prophetic writers after the last verse of the last chapter of Revelation. There have been countless writers, both inside and outside of orthodox Christianity, who have actually given me as good (or maybe even better) understanding of God and helped me experience deeper devotion than Paul and his contemporaries. God is lord of all ages, not just Bible times. It just makes sense to me and, frankly, that's all that matters.

Think about it. Faith based on common sense and supported by scholarly investigation is better than that built on legend, tradition, superstition, ecclesiastical politics and wishful thinking. I depend on my God-given rational senses. I have faith in which they have pointed out in nature and through the insights of intelligent thinkers and the "still small voice of God" within the depths of my own soul. In any context this contribution has stood the test of time. My faith doesn't need to be propped up by cute stories that appeal to immature hopes, dreams and fantasies. Like the apostle Paul, I too put away childish thinking when I became an adult.

I did not say I have not abandoned a "childlike" faith. I have just progressed beyond childishness, although there are times when my behavior challenges that assessment. When it comes to my faith in God, I trust what time, study, experience, education, inspiration and faith have revealed to me more than a childish acceptance of what I want to be true as opposed to what I know to be true. God has given me "response-ability." It has improved with maturity. It has helped me gain that which I didn't have when I was a child, a teen, or even a young adult. In the context of my life, it only makes sense that God and I have established a personal, adult relationship based on the natural ability I have as a human being to observe a situation and use the human brain, which separates me from the animals. I moved beyond a childish mentality and attitudes when I learned to read more than just words on the pages of the Bible. I attained a more mature spiritual understanding when I began to find the truth between the lines and behind the scenes of Holy Writ. I appreciate the stories that influenced me in my youth, but I came to treasure the contextual enlightenment that I got when I discovered the times in which they occurred; the political, social, philosophical and theological climate that influenced them; the audience to whom they were directed; the motivation of their authors and many more contextual influences. As I grow older, then, I depend more on faith and less on religion.

One of the many insights I have gained since I began to maturely search the Bible and my soul for God's truth is that profound things seem to be found in groups of three. I found that an equilateral triangle which holds nine other equilateral triangles can be the depository of my personal spiritual credo. It's a nice fit for what I have come to believe represents my personal faith and religion. I did some research on numerology and found that the number three often—especially in Eastern and Middle Eastern religions—refers to the deity. It is one of the two digits that make up the "complete" number, which is seven. The other number that makes it complete is four, the earthly or human number. When the divine (3) and the human (4) come together there is to be found completeness (7), not good luck, as is commonly suggested. I don't think luck has anything to do with it; faith does. Maybe this is rationalization. I don't know, but it makes sense for me.

So, when all of the more important insights I have accumulated over the almost seven decades of my life began to fall into lists of three parts, I paid more attention to them. All I have to support this is the testimony of scholars who have experienced the same phenomena and the repetition of it in my studies. At this point, faith enters into the equation. There is little beyond the observations of others and myself upon which to base this finding. There are no scientific proofs, nor are there any mathematical formulas to substantiate them. And yet, my common sense within the context of human experience over hundreds of generations seems to confirm that which I would die to defend. It has been good enough for so many of my ancestors; it should probably be good enough for me. You will have to come to your own conclusions.

If you observe my triangle of faith, knowledge and understanding of God, you will see that the names of God traditionally used by the Hebrews, the Muslims and the Christians make sense when put together in the long established cluster of the three each of us has. Yahweh (Exodus 3:14 Allah (Koran) Abba (Mark 14:36 and Romans 8:15) translates into a message from God more than just a name like mine or yours. It says to me, "I AM The God (your) Father." This combination makes sense to me. I have hopes that the religions represented would find in Jesus Christ a unity that would abolish the enmity that has existed among them since the days of Isaac and Ishmael and Jacob and Esau. It just could be that God has hoped that Judaism, Christianity, and Islam would find the fulfillment he expected would come from the covenant he made with Abraham several millennia ago. Common sense tells me that the longevity of the religions that trace their beginnings to Abraham seems to support my observations.

God and Abraham agreed that God would bless the Patriarch's descendants *if* they would bless him. (Genesis 12:1-3) The Jews, the Muslims and the Christians represent those descendants today. We have failed to fulfill our part of the bargain. We have not been the blessing for God that we could or should have been. When Jesus told the young Jewish lawyer that the greatest commandments were to love God, love each other, and love oneself (Luke 10:27), he verified the Abrahamic Covenant. (Genesis 12:1-3, 17) I find that in each of the three Abrahamic religions, a way to God can be found and devotion for him can be practiced. The fact remains that you have an obligation to fulfill what Abraham and God agreed as to what our role would be in his world. And, as a Christian, you have a responsibility to fulfill what Jesus commanded in order to do your part.

I didn't dream this up. The Bible, in the context of the ages and the many people involved and my understanding came together under the direction of a higher and Holy Spirit. Christianity proclaims the Father, the Son and the Holy Spirit (Matthew 28:19) to be the three persons (personalities) of God. We believe that this triune God is above and before all gods. That also stands for the persons who are known to us through the Trinity as Creator, Redeemer and ever-present Counselor and Comforter. Christians acknowledge Jesus to be God incarnate. They accept him as the Son and the Redeemer. He referred to himself as the Way, the Truth and the Life. (John 14:6)

A few years later a man who thought Jesus was a heretic repented and became Christianity's most famous missionary. He was led by a compelling common sense and an overwhelming faith in God to bring hope to all the nations, not to just the sons of Israel. He was Saint Paul and he is quoted as saying, "Believe on the Lord Jesus Christ and you will be saved." (Acts 16:31) He urged believers to do so by power of the love Jesus had commanded his disciples to have for one another. He said it was better than speaking in ecstatic tongues or having prophetic powers and understanding all mysteries. He said that having the love of Christ was more significant than even having faith enough to move mountains. His best known piece ends, "So, faith, hope and love abide, these three, but the greatest of these is love." (I Corinthians 13:13)

Each of these trilogies that I have mentioned has sensitized me to some great contemporary writers. They too have been inspired by the same God who inspired Paul and the others who contributed to the Bible as we know it today. Two of them are Reinhold Neibuhr and Richard of Chitester. Neiburh's "Serenity Prayer" has given millions of substance abusers strength to defeat that which would destroy them. He prayed for *serenity* to accept that which cannot be changed, *courage* to change that which can be changed, and *wisdom* to know the difference. He thought "three" and so did Chitester, a writer of the middle Ages who prayed, "Day by day, O dear Lord three things I pray; to see Thee more clearly, to love Thee more dearly and to follow Thee more nearly." His threefold prayer has been mine ever since I first heard them in the rock opera *Jesus Christ Superstar.*

I too have asked God for the same three things. I too desire to understand him. I desperately want to abide in his presence. And I too hope passionately to know him intimately. I'm sure you could find similar insights if you would only take the time and commit yourself to Chitester's dream. All it takes is what Saint Paul said to the Corinthians. It takes faith, hope and love. In the meantime, I plan to continue my search within the realm of Commonsensible Contextualism. I will bask in the glory of my God's daily presence and dream for the day when I am swept up by his love and transported from this life to that place he has gone to prepare for me.

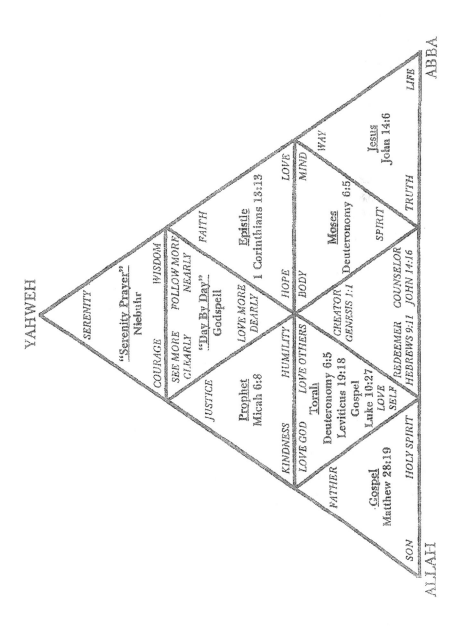

SEVEN

The Fruit of the Tree of Divine Common Sense
Read Psalm 1, John 15 and Galatians 5:16-26

"I think that I shall never see a poem lovely as a tree," wrote the poet. There are those who never get to see the whole forest because they are too busy studying individual trees. With this in mind, I am designing (always present tense) a medium that helps *me* put into focus *my* faith; one that facilitates *my* discovering just what makes up *my* religion. It's a tree grown from the seed that is the pyramid of trilogies I mentioned in the previous chapter. I want to keep in mind that I can't ignore the forest because I have come to appreciate my particular tree. I need to be sure that I relate to yours and those of our fellow citizens within the context of the woods of common sense. Each of us needs to observe the surroundings or the context of our lives. It helps us appreciate our individual *trees of faith, knowledge and understanding of God.*

I believe God has led me down a path of discovery unlike that of some other Christians who see only their particular brand of faith and practice, who either fail to see or refuse to see that God reveals himself in a multitude of ways within the human race's broad spectrum of races, cultures and religions. If it weren't for each tree there would be no forest. But unless one appreciates the whole, the sum of its parts will fall short of giving a true picture of the glories of God's great forest of faith. If I hadn't held this belief I don't think I would have been able to fulfill the demands of my ministry as a hospital chaplain. I have no doubt that it was God's call to minister to each individual *at his or her level of need* that made my work a success. I am also convinced that it was this attitude that witnessed to my Christian faith.

Commonsensible Contextualism simply says, "I am who I am." The Bible tells me that I have been created in the image of God and his name is Yahweh, "I AM Who I AM." I have found that too often many of my fellow Christians have created God in *their* image rather than accepting that mankind is created in *his* image. God is the father of *all* human beings, not just those who choose to mold him into the provincial Being who matches their definition of whom they think he should be. That's why I choose, at this late stage in my life and career, to share my personal faith and hope you will accept my challenge to deal with *my* thoughts, feelings, understandings and beliefs. I hope you will let them become a part of yours. In so doing, maybe you too will come to where I am and understand for yourself the common sense context of God. Who knows, maybe you will grow your own special tree.

When you take time to contemplate the essence of something, it helps you appreciate the value of that which surrounds it—its context. The whole is greater than the sum of its parts. It is more than roots, trunk, bark, branches, leaves and fruit. It is shade, beauty, fuel, furniture, paper, houses and many other things skilled craftsmen can create. Its essence is only partially fulfilled by itself. It takes a forest to enhance its individual trees and their singular contribution to the world. *My* tree, *my* faith is only fulfilled because *I* live it in the presence of *many* peoples, *many* religions, *many* faiths and a God who loves them *all*. To merely observe a single tree and let it go at that is not good enough. Feelings and insights and symbolism can broaden the context of that which one merely means when he or she says "tree" or "me."

Are you with me so far? I know that there are many who think it heresy to even consider the substance of different faith as being equal to theirs. I have served Jesus Christ all my life and I believe that he is the Way and the Truth for my salvation. His blood, I believe, has purchased my eternal soul. To know him is to know God and that, my Bible says, is eternal life. I know that the Jesus I worship, serve and trust never turned his back on anyone, even those who "knew not" what they were doing. He said, "Whosoever comes to me, I will in no wise cast out."(John 6:37) And yet, I have seen his truth revealed in many more ways that that which I learned at my mother's knee, in my Sunday school, and in my seminary. I have seen God reveal himself to Jews, Muslims and Buddhists. I have heard words of faith come from the Native American and the Aborigine. They see God but they see him differently. They see their tree and I see the forest in which they stand.

All of this is prologue for the rest of this chapter. I want to introduce you to a symbol that I have found helps me express my personal faith in God. The sum of its parts is more than my religion. It is the essence of my faith. The fruit that it bears will be my eternal legacy from God. He has given me the insights I will share with you; hopefully they will be seeds that will grow and produce spiritual fruit in you. All this is dedicated to the glory of God and to your intimate knowledge of him. The product of my symbolism can be fuel for energizing your soul and mind. It can be that from which a heavenly home is built. It can be fruit that reveals your repentance. It can be the strength you get from Satan's resistance. It can be the breeze that represents the breath of God.

At the end of this chapter is a diagram of my tree. I believe sincerely that God has revealed it to me. It has been growing out of the depths of my soul and into my mind ever since I was a child. Every year, new—and, I think, better—fruit appears because he is always expanding and growing within me. It has overcome the natural obstacles of my ego as well as that which has tempted me; the sin to which I have fallen prey. As a tree overcomes the crust of the earth, storms, drought and disease, so I have worked hard to overcome the great barrier between me and my God. That barrier is *me!* Truly the words of the psalmist ring true in this case: "The strength of life is labor and sorrow." (Psalm 90:10)

My tree is productive for me because the divine Husbandman has seen fit to fertilize it with truth and the holy influence of family, friends, teachers, the Church, experience and his Holy Spirit. If I have any strength, it has come from hard work and personal discipline. I have had to contend with the thoughtful and concerned beliefs of those who do not agree with me. I have also had to yield to the pruning of some of my thoughts because they were found to be wayward, incorrect or displeasing to the God who inspired me to take on this discipline in the first place. I know that he loves me and understands my goals and my faults and tolerates my frequent ineptitude and failures. So I press on to the goal of greater and more intimate knowledge of him within the common-sense context of his creation and his image.

A tree is just a tree until you make it an object of your study. The tree that is my symbol of faith and religion has been a personal project for a long time. What you see is actually who I am; what you grow will become who you are. When I'm gone to be with the Lord of my life in that place he has prepared for me, I hope it will be an object that will cause people to recall me and say, "He was a good man. He loved his Lord and served him with all of his body, mind and spirit and he loved others as much as he loved himself." I have worked to produce fruit that gives glory to my God and honor to his Son and service the Holy Spirit within a context of common sense.

My tree is rooted and grounded in love. (Ephesians 3:17) It draws from the ground that is God from whom it gets its nourishment and strength. Its leaves have the three segments about which I wrote in the previous chapter. In the Bible, the word "vine" is sometimes used instead of "tree." For example, in John 15, Jesus said, "I am the vine and you are the branches." He goes on to develop the symbol by saying that God helps it bear fruit with nourishment and discipline. The harshness of pruning is as necessary to a tree as physical, mental and spiritual discipline is for the full development of the human being. Like a tree, prayer demands time, thought and discipline. Understanding Holy Writ and faithful service in Jesus' name similarly demand an offering of time, talent, and physical, mental and spiritual energy. Jesus taught that a follower should be willing to go so far as to lay down his or her life in pursuit of fulfilling the call to be a Christian and reap the rewards of the Father's blessing: "Well done, good and faithful servant." (Matthew 25:21)

As Jesus Christ was willing to pay this price, so too he asks us to do the same. Productive lives produce healthy fruit only when they respond to discipline and proper nourishment. The results can be found in a list Saint Paul calls the "fruit of the Holy Spirit": love, joy, peace, patience, kindness, goodness, faithfulness, gentleness and long suffering. (Galatians 5:22) If you ponder these blessings, you will discover that they are twofold in nature. One aspect is that God will heap them on the person of faith; the other is that the person of faith will pass them along to others in God's name. Now there is bit of divine common sense for you! The seed of the Holy Spirit gives and enables. What a genius is our God!

The writer of Psalm 1 realized this and was gifted by God to beautifully pass it along to us. He said that the wise person is one who is willing to listen to God and to godly people and who takes the time and makes the effort to study diligently God's law. He said that such people are like trees planted by a river, whose root system is nourished by that which is essential for growing a productive life. Without drawing strength from the earth and God, man will have no roots from which to grow and sustain eternal life. Jesus told the woman at the well that he could give her "living water." (John 4:10) Trust me, if you irrigate your spiritual roots with *the* Living Water you will grow, strengthen, and produce much fruit worthy of the Divine Husbandman. In Christ you have all the nutrients you will need to grow and produce a life worthy of his effort and grace. But never forget, like a good husbandman, he also prunes or disciplines those he loves in order for them to be as productive as they can possibly be.

No pain, no gain, is as true spiritually as it is athletically. The strength of life *does* result from hard work and personal discipline. The Bible is true to itself. It is consistent because the Holy Spirit who has inspired it is consistent and wise and awesome. Its words are the stuff from which your life can be fruitful and will multiply God's blessing within the context of your total being.

The context of God's Word is great. From a simple tree we can learn so much and we haven't even scratched the surface of what the

Bible and the Holy Spirit reveals. The Book is a never ending source of wisdom and grace flowing from a multitude of symbolic and natural sources. If you choose, as the writer of the Epistle to the Ephesians said, to be "rooted and grounded in love" you will have "the power to comprehend with all the saints (true believers) what is the breadth and length and height and depth and to know (intimately) the love of Christ which is beyond (intellectual) knowledge [and] that you may be filled with all the fullness of God." (Ephesians 3:17f) In other words, you will have been born again because of the intercourse between you and Christ. Conceived in you will be a new spiritual life and through the plan of God and, in due time, a born-again believer who will bear fruit in God's orchard and give glory to his name.

If your roots are in Christ, they will bring nourishment from the ground of all humanity—God himself. From this the trunk, your faith, will be that upon which your tree (life) depends for support and will be manifest in fullness and completeness. James said that we should be joyful when we are tested because the testing of our faith produces steadfastness and that when that is fully developed we will be complete and lack nothing. (James 1:2f). So from the trunk of your tree will come the steadfast branches by which you will bear fruit that will make you known to God and the world, and you will be fulfilled in every sense of the word.

My faith is nourished by *the* Living Water drawn through the divine roots of God's love and supported by my indomitable faith in Jesus Christ. I am a branch born again by the power of the Holy Spirit and I will bear fruit to the glory of God in spite of myself. By the grace of God and the faith of me, I am who I am.

THE TREE OF FAITH, KNOWLEDGE AND UNDERSTANDING OF GOD
FROM THE HEART OF A "COMMONSENSIBLE CONTEXTUALIST"
(Rooted and grounded in the word of God)
(ephesians 3:17)

YAHWEH
(exodus 3)
ALLAH - ABBA
(koran) and mark 14:36)
FATHER - SON - HOLY SPIRIT
(matthew 28:19)
CREATOR - REDEEMER - COUNSELOR
WAY - TRUTH - LIFE
(john 14:6)
LOVE GOD - LOVE EACH OTHER - LOVE YOURSELF
(luke 10:27,28; leviticus 19:18; deuteronomy 6:4,5 & matthew 25:31ff)

BODY	JUSTICE	FAITH
MIND	KINDNESS	HOPE
SPIRIT	HUMILITY	LOVE
(deuteronomy 6:5)	(micah 6:8)	(1 corinthians 13)
SERENITY	SEE MORE CLEARLY -	UNDERSTANDING
COURAGE	FOLLOW MORE NEARLY -	PRESENCE
WISDOM	LOVE MORE DEARLY -	INTIMACY
(reinhold neibuhr)	(richard of chitester)	

GENESIS 1:1; 12: 1-3 and 32.28
DEUTERONOMY 5:6-21
PSALM 1 and PSALM 90:10
I CHRONICLES 4.10 and II CHRONICLES 7:14
MATTHEW 5,6 & 7
JOHN 1:1   JOHN 4:21   JOHN 17:3
ROMANS 12 I CORINTHIANS 13 GALATAINS 5:26
JAMES 1:2-8   REVELATION 3:20
THE KORAN, THE BAGHIVAH GITA, THE TAO TE CHING
ETC., ETC., ETC.

EIGHT

Roots

Read: Ephesians 3:14-21

"Jesus makes sense!" I believe it. I trust my eternal soul to its wisdom. Within the context of all creation these three words build, maintain and sustain my relationship with God. They underscore that which I have preached and lived for a lifetime. From the roots to the fruits of the Tree of Commonsensible Contextualism, these words say it all. Jesus makes sense. I believe it and, for me, that settles it!

I remember the day that this phrase grabbed my attention. I was cutting the grass in my front yard when a church bus drove by. I noticed that painted boldly on all four sides were the words "Jesus Saves." They were words I had seen many times and in many places over the years. I sincerely believed them, but on that day, I asked myself, "If I owned a church bus, what would I paint on its sides to witness for Christ and promote my church?" The answer came to me plainly and naturally and has evolved into all that this literary effort has come to be. There wasn't a flash of lightning or a choir of angels, just the hum of the lawnmower and the peace that comes when you have a moment of spiritual insight. I thought to myself, "I know—I'd print 'Jesus Makes Sense.'" It was no big deal, but to this day I remember this simple revelation which has dominated my heart and soul and influenced God's call on how I approach my witness and ministry in the name of Jesus Christ. It has come to be the foundation for my understanding of how God wants me to address the needs of those who hear my sermons and the sick, suffering, dying and grieving to whom I minister. It is the basis for my fundamental understanding of God as he reveals himself through common sense in the context of my personal life and the world in which I reside.

This leads me to the subject of this chapter: the *roots* of the tree of Commonsensible Contextualism. Whoever wrote Ephesians 3:14-19 (tradition says Saint Paul, but scholars aren't sure) said, in so many words, that he or she bows his knees before God in order to acknowledge that he is the Father of humanity. From him comes every family on earth. He goes on to testify that from God's treasury of wisdom is granted inner strength to those who believe. It is the "peace that passes understanding" that Saint Paul talks about in Philippians 4:6-7. There he wrote, "Don't worry, pray about everything and fill your supplications with thanksgiving. Honestly tell God what you feel and the result will be the peace that is beyond your human comprehension." The Schofield Bible says that such inward peace is one in which the believer has committed all anxiety into the hands of God through prayer and supplication with thanksgiving. It is an emphasis on the quality of how one feels when he or she is "*in* Christ."

Okay, back to Ephesians 3. This peace comes strictly through faith and is the direct result of the influence of the Holy Spirit, who enables the believer to experience within his or her soul the reality of a saving relationship with the Christ. It is natural for a thinking Commonsensible Contextualist to ask "Why?" The answer is given in verse 17, which testifies that you who are rooted and grounded in the love that is above all love can be empowered to intellectually comprehend within the Communion of Saints (the Church) the breadth, the length, the height and the depth. In other words, those of us who accept the love of God in Christ can know everything there is to know about the love which is beyond intellectual understanding. It is given by God's grace to those who believe so they might be filled full in the heavenly Kingdom of God. This grace is the agape love of which the Bible speaks, the love that has no strings, is undeserved and unconditionally given by God, who is the very essence of love.

The roots of the Tree of Commonsensible Contextualism function effectively because of the ground in which they grow. Our tree stands tall and bears healthy fruit because its roots absorb God's love. The roots of Christianity were written out of intellect by inspired Bible writers, spiritually affirmed by the Gospels, and divinely confirmed by the Holy Spirit in the context of common sense in the hearts of sensitive believers, who faithfully transcribed what they believed God wanted them to write. The roots of biblical wisdom and its common-sense fruit stem from words inspired by God and written by human beings. The product of this divine/human partnership is the redemption of the fallen human race and the restoration of the Kingdom of God that was originally experienced in Eden.

The Shema (Deuteronomy 6:4-5) is the cornerstone of Hebrew theology. It says, "Hear, O Israel, the Lord our God is one Lord; and you shall love him with all your heart, and with all your soul and with all your might." That's the Law which the prophets interpreted and preached for centuries and which Jesus affirmed. Luke writes that Jesus acknowledged a second commandment from the Torah that was equal to the first. It directs the faithful to "love your neighbor as much as you love yourself." He sharpened his focus on this truth in the parable of the sheep and the goats (Matthew 25:31ff) when he said, "In as much as you did it unto one of the least of these my brethren, you have done it unto me." It's one of Jesus' most sacred truths: "If you love others, even the least of them, it's the same as loving me." Makes sense to me!

The Bible has a timed-release quality. Its wisdom is released over a lifetime when you are prepared to understand and apply its common-sense wisdom within the context of who you are, where you are and what is going on in your life. You can read the same words and familiar stories over and over but not realize their truth until you have matured and God is ready for you to use them. The truth isn't new. It has always been around. The difference is you have moved into a context in which it makes sense for you and your context. It is just like one of those capsules that has hundreds of tiny pellets that dissolve at different times in order to spread out the strength of the medication and to make it fulfill its purpose at the right time with the right strength.

The Word of God is rooted and grounded in his love so that the human being can be challenged for a lifetime, and its truth and power can be spread out over the times it can make the most sense and provide the greatest testimony to the greatness of God and his wisdom.

Then there is the testimony of the man who thought he knew all he needed to know about God. In fact, he was so convinced of this that he persecuted the followers of "the Way." Saul became Paul after he grew up and matured at the right time and in the right place so God could produce the fruit of the Gospels in the lives of the millions who were and have been exposed to what the future apostle came to understand in his Lord's good time. What is probably the best known of Saint Paul's words sum up the essence of the ground in which the roots of the Christian faith are to be found. He said, "Let me show you a better way. It's better than speaking in the tongues of men and of angels, or prophesying, or understanding, or knowledge of facts, or having faith enough to move mountains, or giving your possessions or your body to be sacrificed to God. It is that which abides; that which lives within you forever. It is faith, hope and love, but the greatest of these is love." (I Corinthians 12:31-13:13) Like fruit from a great tree, it took time, maturity, hard work and discipline for it to reach the ripeness that not only tastes good to the soul but nourishes it as well.

Jesus said on the night before he died that if his disciples didn't remember anything else that he had taught them, they should keep this commandment: "Love one another!" Not long before this, he had told them that there is no greater expression of love for another than for a person to be willing to lay down his (or her) life for a friend. In a matter of hours after saying this, he went out and practiced what he had preached. Today, you benefit from the fruits of his words. Through faith, his blood redeems you; you are safely held in the hands that were pierced by nails that represent your sin and mine; and underneath you are his everlasting arms.

The contemporary anonymous writer of the popular poem "Footprints" says it very well:

One night a man had a dream. In it he was walking along a beach with the Lord. Across the sky flashed scenes from his life. For each scene he noticed two sets of footprints in the sand, one belonging to him, and the other to the Lord. When the final scene of his life flashed before him, he looked back at the footprints in the sand. He noticed many times along the path of his life there was only one set of footprints, and realized that they came at the hardest and saddest times of his life. Bothered by this, he questioned the Lord saying, "Lord, you said that once I decided to follow you, you'd walk with me all the way. But I have noticed that during the most burdensome times in my life there is only one set of footprints. I don't understand why, when I needed you the most, you would leave me." The Lord replied, "My dear child, I love you and would never leave you. During your times of trial and suffering, when you see only one set of footprints, it was then that I carried you."

There are times when we assume God has abandoned us, but if we assess the situation with common sense and in the context of our personal relationship with him, we will realize how close he has been all along. That is the kind of love that is the ground in which the roots of the Tree of Commonsensible Contextualism grow. It makes sense. If you are rooted and grounded in the love of which Jesus spoke, you will survive the tempests of life and the diseases that attack you. If you are rooted and grounded in God's love, you will bear fruit that testifies to your faith and proclaims your salvation and sanctification. God is the great Husbandman whose care and discipline bring forth fruit that yields in abundance the eternal life he has promised to those who believe.

NINE

The Fruits of Freedom
Read Galatians 5:13-24

The Bible says, "The wages of sin is death." (Romans 6:23) Conversely, the wages of righteous faith and intimate knowledge of God is eternal life. (John17:3) It seems to me that both of these statements make sense, so let me ask you this: What should be the context that would influence you to choose one or the other? You are at liberty to choose whichever one you want and this creates a dilemma. Do you want the guarantee of instant sensual, material, economic, social or other personal gratification or do you desire to take a chance that the more demanding sacrificial pathway of Christian behavior can ensure eternal life, a life that cannot be corrupted by the world and which is filled with blessings beyond your imagination, while having no physical evidence of certainty; the one Jesus labeled "poverty of spirit"? (Matthew 5:3) One answer is based on experience, the other solely on faith.

God, in his infinite wisdom has endowed us with the ability to freely and rationally choose our own destiny. I believe he has purposely put us into a context of conflict between good and evil, right and wrong, spirit and flesh. We will figuratively rise or fall, succeed or fail, depending on the free choice we make. The choice is purely up to each of us as individuals. I am sure that God wants us to be saved, but temptations of the flesh are many and powerful. We need help to do what is best for us and the Lord, by his grace, has provided it. He supports us with inspired words and prophets, his Son and the counsel of the Holy Spirit and a multitude of other theophanies. All it takes to realize these blessings is faith, some common sense, and a willingness to exert some effort to know (intimately love) him, the only true God.

My enduring relationship with him has led me to believe that he doesn't expect me to be perfect, only that I faithfully try as hard as I can. I believe this because he is constantly assuring me of his grace and reminding me that my faith will be sufficient to achieve his hopes for me. He continuously reminds me that, in all things, he works for good and if I love and strive to know him intimately, I will spend eternity with him in the paradise prepared for those who have faith in him. That's why the concept of justification by faith makes sense. It has worked within the context of my life and I praise and thank God for his revelation to me in this simple and understandable way. Now I understand why Saint Paul wrestled so passionately with all of this as he wrote his letter to Rome, the one that has done more to establish the superstructure of Christian theology than any other.

The fruit of the Tree of Commonsensible Contextualism can be observed in much the same way as the Tree of the Knowledge of Good and Evil which confronted Adam and Eve in Eden. (Genesis 2-3) Truly there is nothing new in the New Testament. Just the fulfillment of what God has already revealed through the writings of what is com-monly called the Old Testament. For example, Paul's words in the fifth chapter of his letter to the Galatians, when read alongside the Adam and Eve saga, present a similar message that uncovers one of many fulfillments in New Covenant writings that have their seed in the Old Covenant. The message is the same: partake of the fruit of the Tree of the Knowledge of Good and Evil and you will be separated from God. Choose the fruit of the Tree of Life and the *Tree of Commonsensible Contextualism* (italics and insertion mine) and you will be saved to fulfill God's original intent for humanity. Take your pick. It's your *free* choice! Remember, the Tree of Commonsensible Contextualism is rooted and grounded in love and is nourished by the Word of God. The Tree of life is, too. If you choose to consume their fruit, you will succeed where Adam and Eve didn't.

Freedom has always intrigued me. It can be a blessing or a curse; a blessing if you choose to be in harmony with the Lord and Creator of Life, a curse if your choice is offensive to him because it is in harmony with the Lord of Death. For whatever reason, God chooses not to play the role of puppeteer with our lives. Right or wrong, good or evil, we are at liberty to live our lives as we choose, no strings attached. The context of common sense tells me that God's way is best. Then why do so many of us so often choose the opposite? Paul himself wrestled with this dilemma. (Romans 7) He said that he too couldn't understand why he did that which he didn't want to do and not do that which he knew he should. Truly this facet of human life is intriguing, to say the least. Every day the word "Israel" means more to me because I have wrestled with God and myself and truly it has been a source of his blessing for me.

To help me put this spiritual dilemma into a reasonable context, God has led me to the wisdom of Saint Paul that is found in Galatians 5. It is amazing how much I turn to a man for truth and wisdom whom I would probably have feared and may have disliked. Paul was dogmatic and rigid and had little time and patience for those who would cross him. Galatians 5 is potent evidence of the Bible's capacity to help me understand common-sense contextualism. It is a work of a human genius who was inspired by God to help me plot the best course to accomplish his highest hopes for my destiny. Once again, the Lord's choice of prophet reflects his divine wisdom. He chose someone whose faults are similar to ours and to many of our other biblical heroes; people who overcame their weaknesses in order to grasp the blessing of the Spirit rather than the curse of the flesh. There must be great rejoicing in heaven when such an occurrence happens.

Let me explain what I mean. The context is a situation that has prompted Paul to write a letter to a congregation of believers in Galatia, a city in Asia Minor. They were a people known for being impetuous, somewhat fickle and seemingly always on the lookout for new and curious things. At the time this letter was written, the church had been influenced by individuals who preached impure Christian doctrine and were soft on the kind of moral behavior advocated by the Lord Jesus Christ. In short, this was a letter to offset purveyors of perverse doctrine. That's the context. Now let's see the common sense with which Paul addressed the situation.

I direct your attention to the two lists the Apostle presents in Galatians 5:19-23. In them he offers his readers a choice. Keep in mind the symbolism of edible fruit. Freedom of choice can be based on the pleasure derived from the moment of initial taste or on the long-range benefits of the nourishment value of that particular fruit. Observe the options Paul gives. They are based on the end rather than the means. The seeker needs to ask before tasting the fruit, "What do I want in the end; fruit that tantalizes me now or fruit that guarantees an eternal future?" The Apostle has set the table. You must choose the menu. You must answer the question: "Do I choose the satisfaction of sensual and personal pleasure or the glory of heavenly actualization?" You are at liberty to choose which one of these will establish the foundation for your future. After this free choice, your freedom is lost. Either you are enslaved to the flesh or are in bondage to the Holy Spirit. In other words, first you have the choice of direction, then you are bound to the consequences of that choice. Freedom is no longer involved, with one exception: you can choose to repent, change your mind and go the other way. The fact remains that any time you choose the direction of your life, you become the slave or the servant of that choice. Keep in mind, God understands what you're going through and will not abandon you, no matter what.

Having established the context of freedom of the soul, here are the choices you will have to satisfy the flesh or the spirit, the body or the soul, the here-and-now or the eternal. You can choose instant gratification for the time in which you are on this earth or the boundless, immeasurable joys of eternal life in the presence of God in which there is no error or discomfort or threat. One is easily and instantly realized, the other demands faith and a focused, intimate love that is sacrificial and disciplined.

Paul makes it perfectly clear how these contexts differ. His lists make choosing simpler. I didn't say *easier*. Your decision tells God, the world and yourself on whose side you take your personal stand. The leaf of love on the Tree of Commonsensible Contextualism testifies that you are to love God, love others, and love yourself. It is a leaf with three segments and produces divinely enhanced fruit. On the other hand, the leaf of self-centeredness and ego enhancement has only one segment, which is interested in satisfying only one person . . . you. Verses 19-22 of Galatians 5 clearly affirm the fruits of this humanistic mindset of unrestrained egotism, undisciplined sensuality, and uncontrolled behavior. The focus is on personal pleasure, greed, hatred, dissension, rebellion, covetousness, substance abuse, and unrestricted self-indulgence. Paul's inspired words tell us that those who pursue such a lifestyle will not inherit the Kingdom of God.

On the other hand, those who walk in the Spirit of God under the shadow of the leaves of the Tree of Life, Jesus Christ, and the Tree of Commonsensible Contextualism will bear fruit that reflects his Spirit. They will receive unconditional love they don't deserve (grace), joy beyond imagination, peace that passes human understanding and patience that understands their human nature. They will know kindness and goodness unlike any they have ever experienced. They will understand the kind of faithfulness that led God to send his Son to be the price of their sin. They will experience the gentleness that sustains hope and will be blessed with God's long-suffering discipline that gives them chance after chance to get it right, the kind of forgiveness that forgives them seventy times seven. (Forgives and forgets.)

The difference between the two choices—the flesh and the spirit— is similar to two humorous sayings. One says, "I like anything that is illegal, immoral, fattening or expensive." The other sounds like mom's advice about broccoli: "Eat it. It's good for you." The common sense of God's inspired word and his divine grace is just that—it's good for you! The fruit of the Tree of Christian Commonsensible Contextualism is not only good for you now, but will refresh you when you are beleaguered by the temptation of the fruit of humanistic sensuality, heal you when you are infected by the disease of sin, and nourish and sustain you until you are met at heaven's gate by the Lord who is eager to exclaim, "Well done, good and faithful servant. C'mon in. Have I got an eternity for you! It's full of unlimited supplies of the most wonderful fruit, a cornucopia of love, joy and peace." You have the freedom to choose. What will it be; that which satisfies the moment or that which satisfies eternity?

It may sound strange, but I have come to believe that temptation isn't bad. I think it is God's way of strengthening your life so it will be acceptable in his sight. Whether you succeed or fail is not as important as whether you persistently seek his will; if you believe in him, trust him and strive for the intimate knowledge that Jesus prayed for his disciples and you, I pray that you will freely choose to chase that elusive goodness that is God's will until the day he allows you to rest in his eternal Kingdom. The resistance Satan throws at you is a divinely approved means by which you become strong enough to be justified in God's eyes.

Temptation is a tool by which you grow and mature spiritually. Strength comes by overcoming its resistance. You aren't born with this strength. It takes a lifetime of pursuing it and faith in the God whose divine common sense designed it. You are saved by God's grace, through your faith, and faith without the works that show a desire to overcome the resistances of human existence is not good enough. You aren't saved by the works. They only reflect your faith, the fruits of your free will.

TEN

A Fertile Mind
Read: Micah 6:6-9

The hand of God sows the seed from which the Tree of Commonsensible Contextualism grows. The common sense of Jesus is clearly visible in the parable of the sower (Matthew 13), a great story that puts into proper context the simple truth that unlocks many of the mysteries of the Kingdom of God. In it, a farmer went to his field to sow seed. Some of it fell where birds ate it; some fell on stony ground and died from exposure to the sun and shallow soil where it lacked moisture and nourishment. Other seeds fell among weeds and thorns and were choked. But some fell on good ground and prospered and produced that which the farmer had planned. To Jesus, this was like the Word of God that is sown in the many landscapes of the human heart, mind, and spirit. Some of it is ignored and wasted. Some is heard by shallow minds and dries up after a brief period of fruitless thought. Some of the seeds of the wisdom of God find a place in which to take root but before it can be harvested it is choked by sin, self-centeredness, and the many distractions of the world. But there is much that falls on fertile minds and produces an abundant harvest for the glory of God.

The Bible is like a sack in which God puts many of the seeds of his wisdom. Within its pages are the beginnings of holiness. Implanted in its deeper context is the grand design of a power that brings it to fruition in a harvest of redeemed souls. The Hebrew prophet Micah was inspired by God to sow a seed of knowledge into my mind from which I have harvested much spiritual fruit. He said that God has requirements that will ensure the fulfillment of his seeds' potential. He requires that we be just and kind and humble. If you take a moment to think about this trilogy of wisdom, I'm sure you will find it very easy to put it into the context of Christian common sense. Allow it to be a seed that will produce good fruit that reveals the hand of God in your life.

To be just is to be more than fair. Fairness makes the playing field level for every participant in the game of life. Justice makes it abound with equal opportunity. Thomas Jefferson wrote, "All men are created equal." I think he was wrong. We are not equally created. Some of us are bigger, smarter, and more creative than others. Some of us use our hands to create great works of art, while others use them to lay brick and mold steel and dig ditches, and still others of us have ten thumbs and are limited in our ability to manipulate anything with much dexterity or talent. There are those whose voices rival the most beautiful songbird and those whose voices could shatter glass. Some are drawn to the secrets of science and mathematics; others find fulfillment in nature and the beauty that is revealed in human social interaction. Some succeed in business. Some are carpenters, plumbers and truck drivers. Some administer homes and provide for their families. Some lead. Some follow. Some succeed. Some fail. Some are bold; some shy. Some search the horizons while others use microscopes. All of us have our own opportunities to grow and produce that which is fruitful in God's Kingdom and he loves each of us with equal passion and equal hopes for our salvation.

The best definition of justice I have ever heard is the Golden Rule. Like gold, it is valued highly around the world and has become the standard by which justice is measured and evaluated. Its simplicity makes it understandable and attainable. Whether it is put, "Do unto others as you would have them do unto you" or "Don't do to others what you don't want them to do to you," it says, in essence, the same thing. This profound statement of divine wisdom is to be found engraved in the hearts, minds and souls of believers everywhere and for all of recorded time. Jews believe it. Christians affirm it and so do Hindus, Buddhists, Muslims and Taoists.

No matter how you say or pray it or incorporate it into your religion, it still proclaims justice to be a top priority on the list of requirements God has for a full life. It is a principle that has survived the resistances of times and satanic onslaughts. It has endured the criticism of humanism and the challenges of atheism. Just try and get a plaque with these universally honored words affixed to a spot in or on a courthouse in this God-blessed land, even though they are the essence of common sense judicial justice. The freedom that was insured by the Constitution of the United States allows those who believe this to be God's golden rule also allows those who don't believe to express their dissent. Truly the strength of our faith and our democratic principles comes as we work to overcome such resistance.

Like the body, the mind and spirit gain strength as they grow and overcome ignorance and sin, so the land of the free and the home of the brave will get stronger because it will overcome the obstacle of humanism. Here is God's universal principle of strength and growth at work in the context of hard work and personal discipline by those who are called by his Name. The rights of those who disagree with this must be considered as sacred as those who believe them. God will be the Judge. His grace will be tempered by his unique brand of justice and his justice will prevail. In the meantime, the battle between right and wrong must continue until he says it is over. God knows what he is doing. If we live by the motto "In God we trust," his will will be done and we will be the beneficiaries. Why? Because he said so, that's why! It's just the way we are to behave. It's the common sense of the Law and the Prophets. It's also the common sense Gospel of Jesus Christ. It's the way the world was created to be. It all fits. Follow God's commandments and justice will prevail. It makes sense to me!

Secondly, God said through Micah that we must be kind. It is one of the many ways he chose to say, "Love one another." It is one of the top two commandments on Jesus' list. Kindness is a gentle form of that love. Jesus used the same tone when he said, "Blessed are the meek." Now, there's a good word. It's like a seed sown in the fertile mind of a Christian. It's a nugget that marks the context of love from the gold mine of wisdom of Jesus' Sermon on the Mount. Like the principle of justice, so too, the principle of kindness is universally expressed by other major faiths. Compassion is a cornerstone of the religions of the world that have survived the test of time.

People of the twenty-first century need to be careful how they interpret "meekness." The evolution of the language has changed its original meaning. Today meekness means weakness. It is used to describe someone who is reluctant to stand up for what he or she believes in the face of outspoken and threatening opposition. It is often used to describe someone who has no backbone and is devoid of macho manliness. But, in truth, it is a word that means unwavering obedience and the quiet strength that tames the self-centered spirit of humanism. It is the kind of strength Jesus displayed as he meekly stood before Pilate, Herod, the Sanhedrin and the Good Friday mob as he bore the burden of the world's sin. It depicts an attitude with which Jesus faced the cross and submitted to the torment of hell.

Surely the meekness of Christ was looked upon as weakness in the eyes of the Roman Empire's governor. Even today, there are those who have missed the point of the meekness of Christ and have allowed the stereotypical definition of the word to make him appear to be less of a man than he really was. The fact is he was more than any man who ever lived. He was the only man to be in complete harmony with the Holy Spirit of God, in all his glory and with every ounce of his disciplined power. In truth it is the seed planted in Joseph of Arimathea's tomb which sprouted on the first Easter Sunday morning and has grown from that tiny, out-of-the-way place in Palestine to that which surrounds the world and has eclipsed the Roman Empire. It has spread into the hearts of believers who have literally turned the world upside down. It has borne fruit that will save the world from sin. It grows today with the same fervor with which it grew then. God will not allow it to be exterminated.

The strength of the meekest of God's creatures, Jesus, has defeated empires and principalities, ideas, philosophies and movements like communism, atheism, humanism and satanism. This quiet strength is exemplified in the humble faith he has passed on to those who take up his cross and follow in his footsteps. It is the only hope for the world. No atomic bomb, no evil despot, no totalitarian ideology has or will ever defeat it. Kindness moves mountains. Meekness obliterates sin. It is a seed, when sown in the fertile minds of believers in Christ Jesus, and it will produce crops of abundant lives that are rooted and grounded in his love.

The third seed that God sowed through the mind of Micah is humility. Like kindness and meekness, the term humility has not fared well in the lexicon of human expression. In today's world it is the assertive person who is admired and respected. The one who believes in him or herself and who makes the world stop and look at them is the one who appears to carry the greatest influence. In every election year we are bombarded with ads extolling the greatness of people who want you to elect them to be your leaders. They are too often chosen because of how they present themselves on TV rather than how well they can perform their duties. Proof of one's sincerity is directly in proportion to his or her humility. It is the stuff that takes time and hard work to make known because it doesn't depend on hype. It depends on results and character. It only becomes visible over long periods of time; time that too many people are not willing to spend.

Jesus was killed like a common criminal. He was buried and it was hoped he would be forgotten. But those who believed in him sacrificed their egos and their lives and day after day, week after week, month after month, year after year, decade after decade, century after century, and millennium after millennium, have made his mission grow from that seed sown in the garden of Resurrection to where it dominates the world and saves hundreds of millions of souls.

In God's eyes special people are the ones who sincerely, humbly and meekly pray, "Not my will but thine be done, O Lord." In God's eyes they are people who lay down their lives for a friend; they are humble, kind, and just persons who love others as much as they love themselves. In God's eyes they are the special people who reflect his image rather than show off their own. They are those who love the love that is unconditional; that has no strings attached or hidden agendas. In God's eyes, it is the just, the kind and the humble who are energized by faith, hope and love and who will be welcomed as his children into his heavenly home. He may require them to love and respect him, but he will nurture them with his boundless love, patience and wisdom and give them time, opportunity and grace. He will sow the seed of success in their fertile minds with gifts of love, joy and peace. And he will remain eternally faithful, gentle and disciplined. (Galatians 5:23) Those who are rooted and grounded in his love and who use the natural resources of common sense within the context of his Word and good time will produce fruit that will eclipse their grandest dreams.

ELEVEN

All God's Children Have Only One Father

Read: John 4:5-26 & 39-42; Luke 10:25-28;
I Corinthians 1:18-25 & 2:2 and Romans 8:35-39

The older I get, the less I worry about things that used to consume a lot of my attention. Things like making a living, raising my kids and climbing the professional ladder used to keep me awake at night and filled my prayers with detailed, self-centered (but idealistic sounding) petitions. Now I find myself more concerned with seeing God more clearly, loving him more dearly and following him more nearly . . . day by day.

The search for peace, prosperity, and success has, to me, become secondary to enjoying the presence of God who has revealed himself plainly to me from a diverse world of people that is like a mosaic masterpiece. I am far less concerned with being number one professionally and denominationally than I am to being subservient to the God who glorifies me through his Son, Jesus the Christ. The prayer of Jabez (I Chronicles 4:9-10) has been answered over and over in my life. I am truly blessed, filled full and saved by the grace of God.

In this time of heightened nationalism, I have come to appreciate the necessity of setting aside ethnic differences in order to rally beneath a banner of stars and stripes. As a Scotsman, I have greater pride in being an American, and as a Presbyterian, I am more content to be a Christian. I can sincerely acknowledge the beauty and influence of the multicultural fabric that has been woven into my great country and my holy religion. I thank God for the realization that I must set aside creedal differences in order to rally beneath the banner of the cross of Jesus the Christ.

As a boy, raised in the Monongahela Valley of southwestern Pennsylvania, I grew to appreciate the contributions of the many sons and daughters of lands foreign to mine. My father was a physician for the National Tube Works of United States Steel. He took great pride in being able to communicate with workers whose native tongue was not English. He used to brag that he could cuss and swear in twenty-seven languages and dialects. When he died, hundreds of people passed before his coffin and told me how much they appreciated his love for them. They loved him, not because he was a good doctor, but because he treated them as if it didn't matter where they came from or how they spoke or where they went to church.

From this background, I came to value the spirit of religious ecumenism. One of my seminary professors defined it as the "urge to merge." That spirit has infected my ministry ever since. From the day I accepted the call of God's ministry in the sanctuary of the Kephart Memorial Evangelical United Brethren Church, I have tried to witness to the broadness of God's grace and the blindness of his love to race, sex, nationality and religion. My resume indicates that I have been a pastor in not only the Evangelical United Brethren denomination but also in the United Methodist and United Presbyterian churches, too. I even served a two-point rural Lutheran parish. I have had the honor to be the first non-Roman Catholic chaplain ever hired by the Sisters of Mercy for Mercy Hospital in Pittsburgh and the founder of the Pastoral Care Departments in three other secular hospitals. I have been designated a Master Catechist by the Roman Catholic Diocese of Pittsburgh, which enabled me to teach people how to minister to the sick, the suffering, the dying and those who grieve for them and how to deal with some of the many crises that manifest themselves within families.

Through all of this, I came to realize that all of God's children have only one Father and he doesn't particularly care about their religious, ethnic, racial, philosophical or economic labels. When a person is sick, suffering or dying, or if someone is sitting at a bedside holding the hand of a loved one, it really doesn't matter to God to what church they belong, or if they belong to a church, or how they recite the Lord's Prayer, or whether they follow an ancient liturgical tradition, or if they make it up as they go along. He could care less if they sing traditional hymns to the sound of a grand pipe organ or contemporary gospel music accompanied by the strumming of a guitar backed up by an electronic keyboard and drums, or if they are led by a song leader who lines out the words of the "oldie goldies."

All that matters is that there is a God who loves them and who walks beside them through the shadows of adversity and who even picks them up and carries them across the troubled waters of dying and death. Denominational loyalties and liturgical practices become blurred by the tears of love and become invisible to the Creator, Comforter, Counselor and Redeemer. "God so loved the *world* that He gave His only begotten Son that whosoever believes in Him shall not perish but have everlasting life," so says the Gospel of John 3:16. Even the rigid and dogmatic Apostle Paul, whose legacy is the architecture of the Church and the basis for many of the traditional practices of that faith said that all that really matters is that we preach "Christ crucified and risen from the dead." (I Corinthians 2:2)

God loves you and acknowledges human differences. He has encouraged religious diversity in order to make his witness fit the needs of the many varieties of people and cultures and traditions that exist on this planet. He gives each inhabitant freedom to choose an individual pathway to his throne of grace. As a chaplain, I was always aware of the richness of all religious traditions. It helped me understand that God is in tune with the fact that when an individual is confronted by life or death, joy or sorrow, love or hate, pain or pleasure, there is nothing that can separate that person from the love of God as manifested through Jesus Christ. (Romans 8:35-39) I can minister to Jews, Muslims, Hindus, Buddhists and Jehovah's Witnesses and I can minister at their level of spiritual need and not compromise my Christian faith. I can respect their faith and religion in the same way that Jesus ministered to a Roman centurion, a Pharisaic lawyer, a Samaritan woman, and an agnostic thief. I can serve those who don't share my religion because Jesus' parents accepted gifts from Persian wise men and instructed us to render unto Caesar the things that are due him in the same way we render unto God the things that are due him. I never cease to be amazed how Jesus' Gospel was built on the solid foundation of faith and common sense.

When Jesus encountered the Samaritan woman, he treated her with love and respect. Her neighbors had shunned her because she lived with a man without being married to him. He was not influenced by her sex or nationality or the way she worshipped God. He was concerned for her eternal soul. He told her it didn't matter if she worshipped in the Temple at Jerusalem or on the holy mountains of Ebal and Gerizim in Samaria. He also told her that true worship was and would be in "spirit and in truth." Then he sent her out to be probably the first Christian evangelist. Before Peter became Pope or Paul became an Apostle or before James and John would sit at the right hand of Jesus or before Francis or Luther or Wesley or Knox became important, this nameless woman was commissioned to tell others about Jesus the Christ. He accepted her and died for her as much as he did for any other Christian luminary or for any bishop or preacher or member of the multitude of alphabetical denominations we belong to, such as the RCs, UMs, UP (USA)s, the LCAs, the ELCAs, the UCCs, the CMAs, the AGs and the *etceteras*. He died for us all no matter what our label and whether we accept women or even homosexuals to be ministers.

I know this is a controversial way of thinking, but I am inspired by the fact that Jesus never ran away from anyone or anything. He stood tall with his controversial thoughts and actions. He stood solid in his controversial relationships. He never walked away from conflict. He had a mission and social popularity was not a factor. He never turned his back on anyone who came to him. The woman at the well was condemned because of her lifestyle. How many lifestyles are unacceptable to you? Ask yourself, "Would Jesus turn his back on a homosexual?" I think not. He didn't to a thief, or to someone charged with adultery. He touched lepers and addressed the personal needs of those who were shunned by society for being insane. He ate with sinners and allowed a woman of sinful reputation to wash his feet with her tears. It got him into conflict with the religious right of his day and it hasn't changed for those who would try to follow in his footsteps today. Pharisaism is as alive and well in the twenty-first century as it was in the first.

Jesus told the young lawyer that the greatest commandments were to love God with everything he had and to love his neighbor as much as he loved himself. He was adamant when he told this Pharisee that if he abided by this code, he would live forever with God. Then he went out and laid down his life for those Pharisees who rejected him, those Romans who didn't know him, those hateful religious leaders whose personal pride and status were threatened by him and for every human being that would ever live on the face of the earth. His blood was shed and his body was broken, no matter if that young man had been a Pharisee, a Sadducee, Roman, Greek, a Christian, a Jew, a Muslim or a Buddhist, a Lutheran, Methodist, Presbyterian, Baptist, or any other special religious interest group you can think of; even an atheist, agnostic, liberal, conservative, or moderate.

The Body of Christ has many members, just as your physical body has many parts. Each has an important function to perform. One is of no greater importance than another. Just as the heart, the brain or the lungs can't function without the kidneys, the bladder or the bowels, so mainline Christian suburbanites can't function without the independents or those who operate out of storefronts in the slums. All God's children have one and only one heavenly Father and he cares little about their labels. Praise be to him for our diversity and praise be to him for our unity. Praise be to his Body (the Church), whose various parts perform functions that lead lost souls to salvation, ignorant minds to truth, wayward feet to the presence of God, and searching hearts to the Way, the Truth and the Life.

Religious unity will come about only when we are willing to set aside our differences, like Jesus did with the woman at Jacob's well, or the young Pharisee, or the thief who died beside him, or the religious leaders of the Temple and the synagogue, or the multitudes he fed and healed, or the rebellious Saul of Tarsus, or the foolish obsessive-compulsive Peter, or you or me, or anyone with whom he takes the time to share himself and for whom he lay down his life or for whom he was willing to leave his heavenly home. In Christ there is no division.

TWELVE

Here I Stand
John 17:1-5 and I John 4:1-6

The countless controversies within the contemporary Church compel me to turn inward and examine my own personal life and faith. The time has come for me to set aside what others believe and focus on what I believe. It's not that others can't contribute to my faith, but when all is said and done, it is what is in *my* heart and *my* mind that counts. The Bible and common sense, within the context of my life and times, will be my chief source of acceptable answers. I believe God's Holy Spirit speaks to me through its enduring wisdom. I go to it knowing that what I will find can and has been used to promote points of view that often disagree with mine. God knows it frustrates me. Then I realize that this is his way of making me come to grips with that which makes him come alive in me. He has shown me that strength will come from willingness to discipline myself; to discover the goals he has for me. I am grateful for his way of having me overcome the resistances and obstacles he has allowed to get in my way. It will be the reason I am strong enough to succeed. He doesn't drop answers into my lap; I have to work hard to find them, just as one seeks buried treasure. I may not like it, but, if I have learned one thing in my life, it is that the *Bible makes sense!*

On the night before he died, Jesus gathered his disciples in the Upper Room. During the most passionate moment, he prayed for them and for us. Part of that prayer went like this: "Father, my hour has come. Glorify me that I may glorify you. (Abraham's Covenant, Genesis 12:2) You have given me power over all flesh that I may give eternal life to them. And this is eternal life that they *know* you, the only true God *and Jesus Christ, whom you have sent.* (Italics, John the Gospel writer) In this prayer, as recorded in John 17, Jesus defined eternal life as "knowing God." It is important that you understand that the term "knowing" is to be used in its most intimate sense. It isn't all together cerebral or intellectual, nor is it casual. It is to be understood as so intimate as to conceive a new life. I know my God so intimately that I have embraced him and allowed his seed to penetrate my soul and conceive within me a new being. I have been born again through the power of this intimate knowledge and I will dwell forever within the living context of his divine presence.

I am not saved because I am a Christian or a Presbyterian Christian. I am saved because I know God intimately through faith in his grace. I may practice this faith through a specific denomination but the intimate union of my spirit and God's is what has brought about this miracle and I have become spirit of his Spirit and he is Soul of my soul and we are one. This is not the result of my religion. It is because of *his* grace and *my* faith. It is holy, not religious; it is personal and spiritual, not social, intellectual, liturgical or dogmatic. It has led me to many intellectual, social, religious and dogmatic conclusions. The set of twelve trilogies I wrote about in chapter six was revealed to me more from a spiritual source than a religious one. I believe it came from the mind of God. I think it states plainly and exactly what I believe. I'm not smart enough to have done this on my own. It has been miraculously born into my soul. As childbirth doesn't happen in a moment so the actualization of the sanctified person takes the context of a lifetime to mature. My faith has endured many tests. It is still growing and fulfilling itself within the dynamic context of the relationship that is uniquely the Lord's and mine.

I belong to a religion. I have philosophical and theological standards. I fear labels like "liberal" and "conservative" and "moderate." I'm a Commonsensible Contextualist. I believe God led me to this through something John the Apostle wrote in his first epistle. He clarified his relationship with Jesus Christ. He was happy with what he had become and had written this letter so that his "joy would be complete." That's why I compiled that list of trilogies and I guess the rest of this first (and probably only) literary effort of my life. I want to bring all that I believe into one simple, understandable statement of faith that will satisfy my longing to be one with Christ and to say it in my own words, complete my joy and assure myself that I have done everything I can to know him and affirm my relationship with him.

In the first verse of the fourth chapter of I John, the Apostle said that each of us should examine that which confronts us. He warns us not to believe every spirit but to challenge the good *and* the bad, to wrestle with them and let the Holy Spirit reveal himself. I have and will continue to test that which stimulates my mind and spirit. I will honestly attempt to glorify God with whom I have an intimate knowledge. I am confident that because of this relationship he will not allow me to stray. Only I can do that and with his gracious help, I will do all within my being not to let it happen.

I am uncomfortable with those who judge my way of thinking as not as good as theirs. Not that I am incapable of error; God knows I have my faults. I find it hard to accept the rejection of my relationship with Christ by someone else. I resent being condemned by those who proclaim that their way is the exclusive one true and only religion. There is but one who can say, "I am the Way and the Truth and the Life," and that is Jesus the Christ. The rest of us need to get in line behind him. You will recall that the Pharisees of his day missed the point and the spirit of the Law and the Prophets because they had become so engrossed in the details of their religion and had come to believe that they had an exclusive hold on the way things were and ought to be.

There are Pharisees today who are alive and well and dwelling in our midst in the guise of Christian purists. I do not presume to have the last word on matters of Christian life and faith. But what I do know, I am convinced I have been given by God through his Holy Spirit. I guess I have to stand as vulnerable as Jesus when he said that he was his own witness and felt that the Father was his co-witness. In the thinking of the world, that may not sound very impressive, but I'm not worried about how the world responds to me as much as I am concerned how my God accepts my efforts to know and understand him. Before writing a book like this I had to realize that I might find myself out on a limb and alone. If I were taking myself seriously as a theologian, that might be something, but all I am is what I have written; no more. I am who I am and what I am and I know whom I have believed and am persuaded that he is able to justify my deductions and beliefs whether I am correct or not. That's the beauty of faith. It doesn't have to stand the test of human standards.

My life's anchor is the Good News of Jesus Christ. His is the grace that is all-sufficient for me. All others must take at least second place, and that also goes for Saint Paul, for whom I have the utmost respect. But he is not my Savior. He's just another guy who has wrestled with the same issues with which I am dealing in this exercise of thinking out loud, if you will. Paul was a man whose words have been remembered because Christ was his Savior, just as he is mine. Paul was certainly a brilliant mind and a committed Christian, but like me, he was a sinner and prone to misjudgment. The overwhelming respect he has received over the years indicates that what he says is worth considering. But, he is not Christ and his words are *not* equal to those of the Son of God.

Religion is not as important to me as one might think, given that I am an ordained minister of a mainline Christian denomination. On the other hand, faith is. More and more I have come to believe that the Church is merely a means to an end. The true end of religion and the Church is the personal, intimate faith of the individuals who are its members. The religion and its attending doctrines, traditions, and liturgies have valid foundations in the words God inspired Paul and others to write, but what makes it the Body of Christ is that its members "know God through Christ." It isn't religion that saves; it is grace through intimate faith that saves. The relationship I have with God is *my* faith. I respect yours and that of others. I'm sure God has revealed himself to you with the same grace and intimacy he has to me. I refuse to condemn anyone who is different from me. Likewise, I won't change my faith simply because someone tells me to. Like Luther, I can say, "Here I stand." I believe God knows me, too. It is not political or ecclesiastical correctness that counts, it's personal.

I like the words of the hymn that says, "I know whom I have believed and am persuaded that he is able to keep that which I have committed unto him against that (judgment) day." *I know* God and I *know* Jesus Christ. He has persuaded me, wooed me and we have consummated a oneness through faith. I *know* the depth of my commitment to him and the loyalty I have for him and he for me. On the day I stand before God to be judged, I *know* Christ will be at my side. My faith in his blood will have cleansed me from sin and I will stand before the Lord my God unstained by evil.

What I have written is my personal testimony of the common-sense context of my love for Christ, who so loved me that he died for me. I don't expect what I have said will be the same for you as it is for me, but I hope that what I have said will be the spark that will encourage you to come to know God and Jesus Christ, whom he has sent. I am confident that if you do, one day we will meet him in that place in which there will be no more differences and no more religious controversy. If you take your stand and I take mine, together we will stand with Christ and enjoy eternal justification.

THIRTEEN

A Means to an End
Read: Colossians 1:1-23

One of my favorite authors is Huston Smith, professor of Comparative Religion at San Francisco Theological Seminary. His book, *The World's Religions*, holds a special place in my library. In it he says that religion is a universal phenomenon that has six basic features that are evident in human nature: authority, ritual, tradition, explanation, grace and mystery. Humans have a natural inclination to feel secure when they are directed by an authority figure. Whether this is a person, a set of principles or an institution, we seem to feel better when we are held close and assured that "everything will be alright." We also feel more comfortable when we can rely on a parent, an institution, a government or a belief system to protect us from an unknown, a threatening thought or situation; or that can explain that which is confusing. It has been my observation that we feel better when we are in familiar surroundings. Rituals and liturgies have a great effect on the circumstances that influence our attitudes. These venerable practices have endured the test of time and have proven to be reliable. We have learned to depend on the message of peace, forgiveness and divine acceptance that originates in religious worship.

Closely related to ritual are the many traditions that have found fertile ground in religion. Tradition is like an avalanche: the longer it exists, the bigger and stronger it becomes. The Christian celebration of Christmas is a prime example. What started out to be a minor observance of the birth of Jesus has become a major holiday with incredible religious, social and economic implications. Every year it gets bigger, more humanistic, more commercial and less accurate to the facts and truth of it. The Church tries to be vigilant and protect her members from allowing it to become too secular, thereby losing its spiritual emphasis. All the while the Church promotes less substantial traditions under the guise of making the Holy Family and the holy night more significantly "religious" and spiritually affirming. She is maternalistic and controlling of that which would threaten the religion she proclaims and the faith she professes.

Ideally, the goal of religion is to help believers relate to God, *not* to promote itself and foster behavior contrary to his will. Huston Smith says that it is natural for human beings to seek means by which the unexplainable can be explained. From the very dawn of human history people have sought answers for the question "Why?" Religion seems to come closest to making us comfortable in the presence of a puzzling unknown. Humans tend to believe that there is a higher power in charge of the world, the universe and one's personal life. We like a divine answer for an unanswerable natural question. Even the insurance companies describe natural disasters as "acts of God."

Grace is a kind of love we can contemplate, but it abides beyond our comprehension. We are limited in our ability to grasp it. We live within vulnerable bodies guided by imperfect minds and driven by fragile egos and incomplete spirits. Religion asserts that God has become available to us through this special kind of unlimited and unconditional love that gives life a purpose. Religion does this by revealing God to be the essence of that form of perfect, unselfish love. He is in charge and through ritual and tradition and obedience we acknowledge him. By faith we explain why he exists, how he makes sense out of nonsense and what we can hope for in a never ending future of heavenly peace. Underneath religion's obvious manifestations is the shadow of mystery.

Man acknowledges his finitude but seeks the infinite wisdom and the eternal presence of Almighty God. He doesn't understand the infinite, so he challenges its mystery within the context of his religion. Religious faith helps him confront such questions as "What is beyond the here and now?" or "Is there life after death?" or "What will become of me when my days are over?" Why? How? Who? When? Where? What?

I would like to put all of this into the perspective of Commonsensible Contextualism. We go to church because we are religious, and for many reasons we believe our particular religion satisfies Smith's six basic religious urges. We sacrifice time, energy and economic resources to belong to a congregation of people whose beliefs are mostly in harmony with ours. But as I said previously, the Church or any other religious institution is only a means to that end, not the end itself. The Church is the result of architects like Saint Paul and almost twenty-one centuries of ardent disciples of Jesus Christ. The Church is the result of those six basic features of religion. She is built on the foundation of the Jesus Christ. Judaism, too, must adhere to the same principles and formula. But you need to remember that the Church and religion in general is not the end to which the six features point; they are merely one of several means by which the ultimate end is achieved.

The end we seek in religion is to help us establish a personal relationship with God. Christians find this through studying the Bible; Jews through the Torah, the prophets and tradition and Muslims through the Koran. All they do is enable and equip you to meet God and allow him to become a part of your soul. The responsibility of religion is to explain how God reveals himself and to help you integrate that into your personal life. Religion can be described as God's right hand or revelation in the world today. It is one of the many vehicles he uses to make it more meaningful. It is here for a believer to accomplish what Moses, Jesus, Mohammad, Buddha, Lao Tsu, and Confucius began.

On the night before Jesus died, he prayed that God would help his disciples "know" him. The intimate knowledge that I discussed in the previous chapter is the entrée God uses to consummate his relationship with you. When you are fully soul of his soul and the Church cannot take credit for it, you are born again. The Church can act as a means to that end but the consummation happens within the context of the intimate relationship that happens when you and God fully unite and become as one divine and eternal being. It verifies a manner of thinking that is shared by other non Judeo/Christian/ Muslim faiths that God can be found within the heart, mind and soul of the human being.

I can make my point, I think, by telling a story of two lives that started similarly but ended differently. Both of the men of whom I speak started out seeking God's will for themselves and the people they represented. Both found themselves moving in directions opposite to that which God would have them go, and each realized his mistake. This is where their similarity ends. One chose to repent and to live and let God be reborn in an intimate way so that his life could be refashioned to fulfill a divine plan. The other was so distraught that he "repented" through the futile act of suicide. But through it all, God still loved them both.

I speak of Saul of Tarsus (Saint Paul) and Judas, the disciple I believe is incorrectly called the "betrayer." Both were religious Jews. Both believed their religion would be the answer for the religious, social, and political problems of Judea. Both encountered Jesus Christ. Both thought Jesus had taken a wrong turn in the direction of his divinely ordained ministry. Paul thought Jesus was a heretic whose followers were subversive to the true religion of Judaism. Judas thought Jesus was the savior of Israel but had failed to take advantage of his great personal appeal to the people and his obvious divine power to eliminate Roman domination of the Promised Land and to reestablish the throne of David. Both sought God's will. Both were blinded by their own personal and religious ideas and needs. Both took action to force Jesus to fit their particular plan. Both failed; Paul, because of his misinterpretation of the Law and the Prophets and Judas because of his misguided political hopes for Jesus. Both let the means to the end become the end itself. Both failed.

The difference between the two was that when Paul realized his mistake, he allowed the Holy Spirit to guide him out of blindness into greatness. Judas repented of his mistake, I think, but didn't let the Holy Spirit convert his energy from destruction into glory. Instead he allowed death to win and one who could have been a valuable servant of Christ was lost. The religion of these two men led them to Christ but failed to help them know him with the spiritual intimacy that Christ had mentioned in his passionate prayer in the Upper Room. (John 17) God loved them both even as they walked the path of misunderstanding and error. He still loves them to this day.

He loves you, too, and he loves the Church that has sometimes misinterpreted the divine truth of Jesus and his Gospel. He has ordained her to help fulfill this love. He has stood with her as she has stumbled through the last two thousand years. It is up to you to choose which direction you will go and what means you will use to overcome your human frailty. The Church can help. She is certainly willing and able to be the means to this glorious end. But, she is *only* the means to the end that God has planned for you and the world. Your faith is what will achieve the end that will, in reality, be only the beginning of an eternal life.

FOURTEEN

Think God
Read: Luke 7:20-23 and John 4:8-30,39A

In 1980, the comedian George Burns played God in a movie entitled *Oh God! Book II.* Not only did I find it interesting and entertaining, but I was also fascinated with its insights into contemporary American cultural attitudes about religion and faith. On the surface, the film appeared to be a cute story and a lighthearted criticism of organized religion. Underneath, however, were some common-sense expressions of how people like to build significant spiritual relationships with God. What grabbed me was the screenwriter's understanding of God and God's willingness to relate to all of his children, no matter what their individual parochial preferences might be.

This seemingly blithe film touched on a subject that is important to me—the foolishness of the secular humanistic understanding of God. In the movie, Tracey, a little girl is visited by God. He persuades her to organize a campaign to encourage people to become more aware of him and how much he wants them to be happy. Tracey and her friends come up with a catchy phrase: "Think God." First it touches the community and then sweeps across the nation and eventually around the world.

Somehow the combination of youthful innocence and a simple sentence grab the imagination of millions of people. The plot develops around the little girl's estranged parents and a collection of stereotypical educators and religious and psychiatric professionals who are so impressed by their own individual expertise that they are blinded to the truth of simple human faith. Their reaction to Tracey's claims about her relationship with God leads them to conclude that she is delusional or demon-possessed and in need of institutional treatment or exorcism. Their typically humanistic or religious provincial attitudes about matters pertaining to faith reveal accurately how many in our society observe spirituality and religious faith. There is little or no room for things of a sacred nature, which differs from their preconceived and locked-in concepts. The characters stand on scientific, philosophical or superstitious ground.

The children—and particularly Tracey—aren't interested in theological explanations or doctrinal pronouncements. All they know is that God was like a little old Jewish man, whose respect for them made them feel good about themselves and who showed them that even though they were just a bunch of kids they could make a difference in the world. Tracey's friends went along with her because somehow it made sense to them that God would communicate in such a way. After all, that is basically what the adults in their lives had been teaching them from the beginning in their religious education classes or family discussions about religion. When the common-sense stories of the Bible were given an opportunity to be put into an everyday context, they lost their relevance. In other words, the Bible is good enough for church and Sunday school but not for the "real world."

In the end, God confronts the academicians, the psychiatrists and the theologians, including a TV evangelist, in such a way that they have no choice but to humbly eat crow and acknowledge God's reality. With gentle humor, he works his will in a mysterious way. When his love is allowed to manifest itself through the honest and sincere expression of believers like children, great things happen. Oh yes—the parents reconciled, the professionals mellowed, and they all lived happily ever after.

The story's outcome shouldn't surprise you. Observe the people Jesus gathered around himself. They were people who simply believed that God saw something in them that he could use to change the world. The rest is history. Simple men of nondescript pedigree and limited education turned it upside down because they didn't allow the "experts" to divert the truths revealed by someone they believed to be the Son of God; someone who accepted their individual talents as worthwhile. To this day they have been successful because they take the common sense of the Gospel of Jesus the Christ and put it to work in the context of the world in which they live. Because someone was willing to take the common sense of the Bible and the context in which it was written and put it to work in the context of here and now, lives have been changed, souls saved and the history of the world affected more by this *one solitary life* than by any one other person who ever lived.

What may seem to have been a piece of cinematic fluff has given me much to think about ever since I first saw it. I still enjoy watching it when it is shown on TV movie channels. It helps me take seriously the role of a child who loves God. It reminds me of how Jesus considered children to be the stuff of which the Kingdom of God is made. It has fixed in my heart and mind a profound, life-changing, spiritually enhancing thought—*Think God . . . He makes sense!*

We live in a complex world. For almost two thousand years, Christian scholars have complicated Jesus' simple message. Not so Jesus himself. He told John the Baptist's disciples in simple Commonsensible Contextualistic terms that he had come to help the blind see, the lame walk, the lepers' skin to be cleansed, the deaf to hear, the dead to rise, and the good news of God's grace to be preached to the poor. (Matthew 11:5) If you are like the people in the movie who thought the little girl was crazy, you are also probably part of the masses who have missed the deeper and more significant message of Jesus' words to the Baptist's students.

If you are a literalist, you would have only heard Jesus say that he had come to cause quadriplegics to discard their wheelchairs, those who need guide dogs to paint sunsets, those who can't hear to enjoy a symphony orchestra or a rock band (or even one my sermons), or dead people to walk out of cemeteries. But to those who "think God," there is much more to be learned from the common-sense words of Jesus. If you can see (understand) him in the context of the world he is addressing, then you will be enlightened and enabled to comprehend the world in which you are living. Those who are blinded by their own importance need to see and understand Jesus as he intended them to see, not as they think they should or have been told they should. Those who are deafened by their own talk need to shut up and let Christ's words penetrate their minds and nourish their souls. Those who believe his common sense in the context of his time will have a better chance to find peace, satisfaction, and success in theirs. Those who believe in the way and the truth of the original Commonsensible Contextualist will put his simple Gospel to work in the context for which it was intended and will be born again from a life deadened by sin and misunderstanding and superstition and tradition. They will be cleansed by the blood of the Lamb from the filth of that which separates them from God. They will be freed from the crippling effects of that which would impair a healthy relationship with him.

When you "think God" you think more clearly and with greater understanding of the master plan for the universe within a context of common sense and divine faith. When you "think God" you probably don't think religiously, but spiritually. As Jesus told the nameless woman at the well of Jacob, "God is a Spirit and those who worship him do so in spirit and in truth." God is a spirit, not a religion. When you worship God, you are not worshipping a set of principles or a tradition. You are saved by faith, not by liturgy or stained glass or a magnificent oratorio or a statue or a painting or a preacher's eloquence.

The Church is a community of saints. It is people, not buildings and institutions. Church officials have been commissioned by their peers in the name of God. If they are only political officials with legislative, economic and social duties to perform, it won't be enough, but if they are partners in the context of the mission and ministry of Jesus Christ, they will walk the walk of those who turned the world upside down over the last twenty centuries. Like the woman at the well or like the little girl in the movie, they too can introduce people to God through Jesus Christ. That's all they are really called by him to do. If they succeed within the context of their individual lives, he will succeed within the context of his and those who "hear" and "see" will be saved, healed of the paralyzing effects of sin, cleansed by the blood of the Lamb of God, and resurrected with him and as heirs to the Kingdom of God. Anyone who hears the Lord with spiritual ears and sees his grace with saintly eyes will be freed from earthly inadequacies.

All that the woman at Jacob's well and Tracey did was to go into their hometown and tell people about someone who made them "think God." After the manner of their Master, Jesus Christ, they fulfilled the definition of an evangelist in a most wonderful yet simple way. Some who heard them responded and were blessed. Others ignored what they were told and remained spiritually impotent. Others believed for a while and then fell away after counting the cost of faith. Still others let the environment of a humanistic world inhibit their spiritual growth. Each person to whom they witnessed responded according to their personal abilities and faith within the context of their individual freedom of choice. Those who thought it made sense grew more in faith than in religion. Within the context of their particular lives, they in turn produced great harvests of spiritual fruit and the Kingdom of God grew, and it will continue to grow until God says, "Enough."

FIFTEEN

Gimme a Break
Read: Genesis 3 and John 14:15

In a most ingenious way, God inspired the writer of Genesis to reveal the truth about the creation of the universe, our planet and those he conceived to live on it. When God fashioned the earth, he saw that it was good and decided to populate it with many varieties of animals, birds, fish and his crowning glory, human beings. He did so with the foreknowledge that the humans would need discipline and restrictions or they would self-destruct. At the same time he had a notion that it would be good to allow them to freely accept or reject his will. There are times when I have serious doubts as to whether I like this or not. Be that as it may, he then thought it a good idea to place in the midst of all of this a source for the "knowledge of good and evil," and told his human creatures to beware of its fruit because it would certainly lead them down the garden path to personal destruction and dislocation from the paradise the Bible calls Eden. The bottom line is, God gave us freedom to choose good or evil, right or wrong, his way or that which the Kabbalists believe to be a divinely ordained "opponent or adversary," Satan. Such freedom has a price.

Yes, freedom does have a price. If you choose to obey God, you pay the price of limiting your knowledge, understanding of and participation in things he knows will harm you. But if you choose to taste the "forbidden fruit" of such knowledge, you may enjoy pleasure and prosperity for a while, but eventually you will have to pay for transgressing his common-sense wisdom. There is a price for everything. You can freely choose to be the slave of obedience, the personal discipline of self-restraint, justice, kindness and humility, etc., to satisfy God's requirements for heavenly citizenship. (See Micah 6:6 and Psalm 90:10) To achieve his reward, you will have to obligate yourself to his way and forego the experience of that which the Adversary would lead you to believe are the ways of pleasure, personal satisfaction, success, equality with God, and independence from what Satan calls God's tyranny. The price: alienation from God and eternal separation when your days on earth are over.

God knows this way will harm you. But, always keep in mind, it is a free and unforced choice. He won't interfere. It is completely up you. You can be enslaved to his will and forego humanistic, carnal pleasures, or you can enjoy them and pay the price of alienating him later. Your heavenly Father knows best, but he leaves the choice up to you. Pay now or pay later, but pay you must. That's the way it is. Why? God said so, that's why.

Having said this, God has provided a means of escape from the wages of sin. He offers an olive branch of reconciliation; an eraser of the blot on your record; a pathway to freedom from sinful misjudgment and willful rebellion, an escape clause, if you will. It is the path of faith in the Gospel of Jesus Christ and trust in the sacrifice of his blood. By this expenditure of spiritual energy you can flee the rewards of abused free thinking. By accepting the gift of the blood of Christ, you can acquire the means by which you will eliminate that which separates you from God, *but* you are also free to reject it. Once again, it is up to you. Take it or leave it.

Freedom is an interesting concept. It can be good news or bad, a blessing or a curse. The key is the wisdom of common sense within the context of divinely inspired faith. Pay the price of such a gift and you will end up in paradise with God. Reject it and spend eternity wishing you had made the other choice. To me the saddest words I ever heard were, "If I had only . . ." Salvation is not only knowing God, it is also being able to intellectually and spiritually know the difference between the alternatives he has established. This is the reason the various twelve-step recovery groups begin their meetings with the Serenithy Prayer: "God grant me the serenity to accept the things I cannot change; the courage to change the things I can;

and the wisdom to know the difference." In other words, "Help me know the difference between what is best for me and that which is wrong, then help me to choose correctly." Jesus said that such divine knowledge is eternal life. With incredible common sense he tells us to love God (know him intimately), love others and love yourself. The result is cast in stone or the heart of God, whichever one you prefer: "Do this and you will live." (Luke 10:28) Don't do it and you will slide down that slope that leads to disappointment and eternal separation from God.

I must confess that I am not free from the sin of such abuses. I too have made wrong choices from time to time in my life. I am not free from sin and I am not so self-righteous that I can point the finger of accusation without being firmly aware that I too have fallen under the power of that which would cause me to transgress God's freedom and to make the choices he would rather I had not made. I often find myself crying out to God in the same way Saint Paul did when he said, "I do not understand my actions. For I do not do what I want, but I do the very thing I hate . . . . O wretched man that I am! Who will deliver me from this body of death?"

You might be asking yourself, "What is he trying to say? He has been rambling on about freedom and common sense and sin and pleasure and prosperity. How are they connected?" The truth is to be found in a few simple terms like faith, grace, discipline, personal responsibility and, of course, common sense. To make my point, let us consider the great ideal upon which the United States was built. In America we have certain inalienable rights that promote life, liberty and the freedom to pursue happiness. One of these rights is that of free speech. Sounds good, doesn't it? It is . . . *if* you choose not to abuse it.

Before I go on, let me affirm my characterization of sin. *Sin is not doing bad things; it is abusing that which is good.* In the case of free speech, how can such a beautiful right be sinful? When it is abused, that's when; when it is used to oppose the common-sense wisdom of God. It is a curse when it is abused. It is a blessing when it is not. One of the reasons I chose to write about it is because I can see America sliding down that slippery slope to destruction because of gross abuse of this beautiful right to speak one's mind. If it is abused by preaching irresponsible living or that which is opposite to God's special revelation and discipline for human living, then the result will be chaos like that which existed before he established the human race.

In America we can say just about anything we want to say as long as it doesn't interfere with the rights of others. How then, you ask, can the likes of Hugh Hefner, Larry Flint, and Howard Stern be justified? Why would the American Civil Liberties Union defend the socially, morally and spiritually destructive trash these men proclaim in magazines and on the air? In my mind, they abuse God's commandments pertaining to how we use our bodies, speak our minds, profess our faith, treat other people, and consider the Name of God. These humanistic thinkers have led our culture to the brink of moral decay and we are threatened with the collapse of the family, our communities and all that the Bible, the Koran, the Bhagavad Gita, and the like profess; not to mention God's Commonsensible Contextualism.

They stand on their right to preach that which we believe God has revealed through these holy books to be wrong. And they do so under the protection of the Bill of Rights of the Constitution and within their God-given right to choose the course of their own individual lives. When those of us who believe in biblical principles oppose them, they often complain that we are wrong and that we are stepping on their right to express themselves freely. Well, my friend, I guess free speech is a two-way street. If they can profess smut and sinful behavior, then I can freely say to them, "You are wrong."

They have the right to disobey God and we have the right to disagree when they do. Humanists profess that they should be allowed to freely publish their libertine message and promote their sinful lifestyles and that those of us who disagree should keep silent. They tell us to keep our faith and religion out of the mainstream of our culture and off the airwaves and separate it from the law of the land. They fight hard to have believers restrict expressing their faith within government circles. Frankly, that's brainless. Unless we proclaim the Word and the will of God about such blasphemous and unrestricted loose behavior, it will destroy the land that was founded to provide free expression. Since when is it wrong to oppose lying, cheating, stealing, murder, defamation of character, or the disrespect of parents or moral/religious principles?

Those who would ban public display of things like the Ten Commandments are actually contributing to the decay of our society. Where is their common sense? This is gross hypocrisy. They flaunt the goodness of freedom of speech when they promote degenerate behavior and literature, but when they actively oppose the public display of the Ten Commandments or any other faith-based statements that foster family strength, religious free expression and honest living, they do so in the name of freedom of self expression. And, at the same time, they're right. God and decency will be the ultimate judge. Those of us who choose God's way will have to let them sow their seeds of smut and degradation, all the while doing our best to counteract it and wait for the ultimate judgment from on high.

Gimme a break! If it's okay to preach the abuse of God's moral commandments by advocating sexual promiscuity and undisciplined speech, then why isn't it equally okay to preach obedience, faith and religious expression? The whole situation challenges sound reason. One commonsensible answer that I can think of can be found in Psalm 1. It says that God knows that those who walk in the counsel of the wicked or stand in the way of sinners or sit in the seat of scoffers will be like the chaff which the wind (Holy Spirit) will drive away. They will not stand in the Day of Judgment or abide in the congregation of the righteous. For the way of the wicked will perish. On the contrary, those who meditate on the law of the Lord and who delight in it will be like a tree planted by a stream. They will bear fruit that reflects his will.

God has revealed through the common sense that is found in the context of his divine revelation that the way to eternal life isn't broad and easy. The person who overcomes the many obstacles that are to be found on the highway of life and who is willing to sacrifice self for God and who is energized by faith, hope and love will hear the words, "Well done, good and faithful servant. Enter into the joy of your God."

Gimme a break! Let me believe in God and let me tell the world about him. What harm can I do? I certainly will not threaten or defeat any of the principles of God's creation. I just might keep some free-thinking, unbelieving human being from sliding down the slimy slope to hell. I want to express my thanks for this paper pulpit or soap box and the country in which it is published for the freedom to express myself and for those who just may read what I have written.

Because I have taken the opportunity to exercise my right of free expression, I feel better. It will make me want to get up tomorrow and start all over again telling people that God loves them and wants what is best for them and wants them to make good choices and refrain from abusing that which is good. All the while I will keep in mind that my choice is free and the consequences will be up to God to measure.

In another sense I might actually need to be thankful for this clash of these opposite points of human view. If I am correct, and God has established the need for resistance to bring about strength and growth of character and faith, then by confronting the forms of what I consider to be satanic behavior and philosophies, I should be growing stronger in my resolve to follow the righteous paths established by God in the Bible and other documents of faith like the Koran and Bhagavad-Gita. By overcoming that which is, in my view, not of God, I am stronger and better able to face other experiences that necessitate spiritual strength. Whether I like it or not, facing and overcoming that which is opposite to my principles of faith will make them stronger and I will be drawn closer to God and enabled to serve him and others in a manner acceptable and even pleasing to him. He didn't say life would be easy. He did say that the strength of life will come from the hard work and personal discipline it takes to overcome that which would separate me from his grace. (Psalm 90:10)

I strongly believe that God has designed the world and the human experience to have this uncomfortable even painful intercourse. It is consistent with his reasonable principle of strength and growth that Psalm 90:10 reveals. It is the reason an individual who, by faith in the precepts of God, will strive with all his or her body, mind and spirit to know and love him. It is the reason he or she will summon the energy of faith, hope and love to overcome the obstacles of humanism and satanic temptation to become worthy of being designated an heir to the kingdom of their Abba (Father). It may not be fun but the reward is worth the effort it takes to follow him daily, even bearing a cross if needs be. It makes sense to me: there is no gain without spiritual, mental, emotional and physical discomfort; even unqualified pain. God is great and God is good and his plan is ingenious. Those who would make it complicated have failed to enjoy his wondrous truth. Those who see its common sense within the context of biblical truth and apply it within the context of their lives will find themselves in the realm of love, joy and peace, basking in the patience, kindness and goodness of God and enjoying his faithfulness and gentleness. (Galatians 5:22,23)

SIXTEEN

In God's Name

Read: Exodus 3:13-15 and Psalm 34:1-3

There are in this world some things I *think*, some things I *wish* and some things I *know*. I *think* I understand the nature of human beings. I *wish* I could control that nature within myself and others. I *know* that the Word of God is the key to fulfillment of all these thoughts and dreams. I *know* that there is a God whose name I revere and I *know* he enables me in a very personal way.

For Christians like me, the Bible is the foundation upon which truth, as I understand it, is built. That is why it exists. It isn't a history book, although it includes people, places and events that are important in history. It isn't a collection of biographies, although its message is told through the lives of some of the most captivating personalities you will ever encounter. It isn't philosophy or theology, albeit some of the world's most significant thinkers based their concepts on what they gleaned from it. What it is is *truth* and I *know* that on it you can build a faith that will help you find peace in this life and paradise in the next. It is that against which no power on earth has or will ever prevail. In short, the Bible is a book of truth, not a book of facts. Like the song says, " . . . this I *know*, for the Bible tells me so."

I believe what I have just said with every fiber of my being. The fact that the Bible exists is, by itself, proof enough for me. It has endured centuries of religious and secular criticism. Many scholars have taken their best shots at it and still it stands equal to or above that which science and literature have claimed. The fact that no political power has been able to suppress it for any length of time says to me that there is a Higher Power in the universe who will not permit it to be destroyed. I truly believe that this power has inspired it, promoted it and protects it. God has put me on the right track to understanding it. I *wish* I could say that I *know* that I have succeeded. I really shouldn't say such a thing . . . but I will. I *know* it. Because of this book, I *know* God. Because of the Christ I met within its pages, I *know* him well and I thrill when I read his words, "This is eternal life, that they *know* Thee, the only true God." (John 17:3)

I have spent more than sixty years reading, searching, absorbing and digesting this work of genius. It isn't really the kind of book you feel you can't put down. On the contrary, there are times when I must put it down in order to ponder for hours at a time the truth that a mere verse or two has revealed to me. Like time-release capsules, its truth can be read and reread many times over for years and suddenly something significant that you have never noticed jumps off the page and changes your life. I don't know how many times I have heard Bible students of mine say, after such an experience, "I never thought about it that way before."

It is amazing how much influence this book has. Its wisdom converts the hearts of diabolical criminals. Its authority alters history. It inspires great works of art, music and literature. It soothes the troubled hearts of those who grieve and boosts the courage of common people to uncommon feats of heroism. It is beloved. It is doubted. It is feared. It is ridiculed. It has been banned and burned. Yet it annually leads the list of best sellers in bookstores around the world. It is respected in every culture and printed in every language. Why? Because God said so, that's why! I am sure he would never permit its destruction or allow its alteration or disgrace.

The Bible makes sense! That's why I know what I know about it. Let me give you just one of a hundred possible examples of why I *know* this. Have you ever wondered about God's name? In his name, people have done almost everything: we pray; we dedicate our time, talent and tithes; we affirm our faith and elevate the common to the divine. In God's name we turn acquaintances into marriages and swear to tell the truth, the whole truth and nothing but the truth in a court of law. With God's name we make things special. Conversely, in his name many evil things have been justified. Wars, racial prejudice, religious bigotry are only a few of the wicked things that have been perpetrated under the cloak of respectability and righteousness that comes from putting this name next to what is said or done. Using God's name as a talisman, people believe they will win a game or even hit the lottery. This is solid proof that the name of God is, has been and always will be integrated into everyday human experience. It is against his will that it be vainly used. But sadly, I think most of us use it that way and think little about doing so. I *wish* we didn't, yet somehow I *know* he understands.

God's name is important, isn't it? But how much do we ever think about it? Where did it come from? As you read on I hope you will come to *know* him better because of what the answer to the above questions reveals. An incident in Moses' life is a source for that answer. The scene is one in which God and Moses are involved in a hot debate over the Lord's call of the great leader. He wants Moses to lead the enslaved Hebrews out of a bondage that has lasted nearly four hundred years. Moses doesn't want the job. He has just been confronted by the voice of God, speaking miraculously from a burning bush that is not consumed by the fire. While he is impressed, he still doesn't want any part of going one-on-one with the mighty Egyptian Pharaoh or being the leader of a confederation of quarrelsome Hebrew tribes named after their patriarch, Jacob. Like many of us, he is reluctant to make a commitment. He knows the stubborn nature of the Hebrews and the equally inflexible personality of Ramses, the Egyptian monarch. Add to that the fact that he would be the spokesperson for the even more immovable Almighty God. Now that's a political predicament few if any humans would agree to assume.

At this point, we should remember that Jacob was also known as Israel. (See chapter five.) After an all-night struggle, one that could easily have been brewing for months or years, this troubled, egocentric, spoiled brat was dramatically changed. He had a confrontation with God and the Lord blessed him for his honesty and forthright prayer. Israel means "He who wrestles with God." It was a prophetic vision of the personality of the descendants of this man. Facing God and letting him know exactly how you feel is the kind of relationship he desires. The Jews have always been known for their straight-forward rapport with their God. They know exactly where he stands because he has made them know it is alright to bear their feelings in his presence. Wrestling with God is no sin. It is an honest relationship that brings blessings worthy of a loving Father and a headstrong child.

Even though Moses knew this about his long-oppressed kinsmen, he didn't wish to be the one to facilitate their deliverance and to fulfill that which God had called him to do. As the conversation between Moses and God progressed, the great man asked God, "When I say to these people that the God of their fathers, Abraham, Isaac and Jacob, has sent me, they will want to know your name. They have only known you as El Shaddai [God Almighty] or Adonai [Lord]. They will want something a little more personal. What should I tell them?" To this God responded, *"O my, I never thought about it. I didn't think I ever needed a name. I just assumed they would know who I am . . . Okay, tell them my name is Yahweh, I AM, because I Am Who I Am. That ought to say it best."* (The italics and imagined quotation is mine.)

With that simple explanation, God revealed a great truth: <u>HE IS!</u> It is a statement of truth far more than fact. It takes faith to believe it, not facts. It is all you need to know to build a faith that leads to eternal life. It is the reason Moses relented and accepted the commission to pilot the Exodus. It is the truth that inspired the Hebrews to follow him out of Egypt and into the unknown realm of the future and the wilderness. It is the truth that gave birth to a nation. It is the name that represents the grace of God, which endured their rebellious human nature. It is the name of him who took the form of a man and came to reveal to all the meaning of that holiest of names.

In Jesus, I AM became Emmanuel (God with us). Jesus called God another name: Abba, which means father, not in the formal sense but in an intimate way. To serve his Father, Jesus laid down his life for us so that we too could relate in a personal way to the God of gods and the Lord of lords.

To others, he had other names. Mohammad called him Allah, meaning "The God." Daily, Muslims bow down and say prayers that are prefaced with the words, "There is no God but Allah and Mohammad is His prophet." It's kind of neat how God is revealed so well through these three religions that affirms him in the world. Together they say "I AM The God [the] Father." To me that makes a lot of sense and it flys in the face of provincials that claim that God can only be known in their way and no one else's.

The Bible is not a book of facts. It is a book of truth. Use it to find your personal name for God. Don't let the world or even the Church confuse you. Don't let the facts get in your way. Let the Holy Spirit of Yahweh inform you, enlighten you and lead you to an eternal personal relationship with him. What do you call God? I know what I call him and because he has honored this name I *know* him and am saved by him unto eternal life. He has blessed me with that poverty of spirit that yields ownership of the Kingdom of Heaven. He has blessed me with an attitude of repentance and meekness that forgives my sins and allows me to inherit his earth. I am blessed with a feast of righteousness, his mercy, a purity of mind, body and spirit, the peace that transcends human understanding and his gratitude for my willingness to be vulnerable for his sake and in his name. The Beatitudes have come alive in me because I have called on the name of the Lord and he has fulfilled its meaning within my being. He is and I am and we are . . . one!

SEVENTEEN

It's Not What You Know, It's What You Do With What You Know

Read: Psalm 90 and James 1:2-18

Many times within the context of my life, I have been tested as to what I know. These were the challenges that turned thoughts into strengths and disciplines that produced physical, mental, social and spiritual growth. That's what Psalm 90:10 and James 1:2 mean to me and why these words make so much sense. In Psalm 90, Moses was inspired by God to say, "The strength of life is labor and sorrow." In James' brief epistle, the wise and practical half brother of Jesus was moved to say, "Count it all joy, when you meet various trials, because the testing of your faith produces steadfastness, which, when fully tested makes you perfect and complete and lacking nothing."

Of all the divinely motivated writers who contributed to the Bible, James is the one I am most inclined to call "the patron saint of Commonsensible Contextualism." I believe this first naturally born son of Mary and Joseph possessed the same kind of thinking that has attracted so many of us to his older sibling and who was raised under the guidance of an idealistic mother and a blue-collar father, whose faithfulness is the seed of many Christian legends.

Knowledge is something that is forever expanding. We live in an age in which there is so much of it that we have had to invent a technology that helps us store it in an easily accessible place. The computer enables us to know more and put it to work faster and more efficiently. Our knowledge, abilities and potential are always expanding. God, in his wisdom, has enabled us to fulfill his will in so many wondrous ways.

Ever since the beginning of human history, we who populate this planet have always been challenged with how the gift of free will and independent thinking is to be used. I have come to believe that sin isn't the fault of knowledge but the abuse of it by enlightened human beings. By God's grace, we have been endowed with this awesome gift that sets us apart from the rest of the creatures that inhabit the earth. The Catechism says that we are to use knowledge to glorify God and benefit each other. But you know as well as I do that it isn't unusual for freethinking humans to convert that which is good into that which is contrary to God's Golden Rule of using it for others in the same way we want them to use it for us.

The "intimate" knowledge of which Jesus spoke in the Upper Room is manifest when people of faith utilize the facts they have learned to fulfill the will of God. It fulfills his expectations that we love him and each other as much as we love ourselves. It is easy to understand why we should love him, but if we abuse our love of others and ourselves, we disrupt the balance of his commandment and we violate its intent and offend him.

When I put myself before God, I break the first of his Ten Commandments. It is no sin to love myself, but if I do so at the expense of another person or of God, I sin and separate myself from you and him. Commonsensible Contextualism teaches me to learn from within the *context* of God's Law and then use it in the *context* of my personal relationship with Jesus Christ, the times in which I live and the people with whom I live. There are many ways I can glorify God through the knowledge I have accumulated. At the same time, it will challenge my capabilities and produce steadfastness. Eventually it will manifest itself in perfection and completeness. As James puts it, I will lack nothing.

It makes what I call "the divine equation" come alive. That is, *God* (3): Father, Son, and Holy Ghost; Creator, Redeemer and Counselor plus *me* (4): heart, mind, soul and strength; north, east, south and west; summer, fall, winter and spring *equals completeness (7).* It is often difficult for somebody like me, a man of the modern age, to understand the concepts of Middle Eastern numerology that is often seen within the context of the scriptures of the Jews, Christians, and Muslims and the several other relevant religions of the East.

The pragmatism that exists within the context of the world in which I live too often casts aside such beliefs and the ancient wisdom they mysteriously reveal. The ancients and the mystics very often represented the divine deity with the number three (3) and the human/ earthly with the number four (4). When the two come together they become seven (7) or twelve (12) and signify completeness (*not luck*). When I have God and he has me, each of us is complete. I guess I am too much a person of twenty-first century America to appreciate the wisdom these mysterious beliefs reveal. However, I do acknowledge that there is something I should respect about it all. Maybe it doesn't make sense to me here and now, but maybe someday God will enlighten me as he has so often in the past.

In Micah 6:6-8, the prophet reveals this truth when he urges me to *be* just, to *be* kind and to *be* humble. Like Jesus in the Sermon on the Mount, this prophet reveals a divine *BE-attitude*. Saint Paul works within the same context when he asserts that we should *be* in an *attitude* of faithfulness, hopefulness and love. (I Corinthians 13:13) Am I wise enough to put it into action and let this wisdom come alive in me? It is *not* what I *know*; it is what I *do* with what I know that counts.

Atomic energy is a blessing if it enhances our world and glorifies God, who allowed it to be discovered. It is a sin to use this knowledge to kill, dominate or degrade our fellow human beings. It is a blessing if it builds or improves the quality of our existence. Likewise, drugs aren't bad; it's their abuse that is wrong. Alcohol, food, money or sex aren't bad, either, it's their misuse that disrupts the balance of what God created in the world. In creation, God gave us everything we need to be happy, knowledgeable, and wise and everything we need to please him. He has also enabled us to freely choose to ignore this wisdom and abuse all that he allows us to know. It is a challenge that strengthens and enhances our minds and spirits, glorifies God and benefits mankind.

A word about the alternatives God allows to happen. So much unhappiness and pain and suffering seem to be within God's providence. Why? Does he enjoy watching us squirm and suffer? If he is such a loving God, why does he allow so much pain and unhappiness to occur? In the movie *Oh, God! Book II,* God and the little girl who is the central character of the film are walking along and she asks God, "Why is there so much pain and unhappiness in the world? Why won't you change it?" To which God replies, "I can't change it." She is perplexed and says, "You're God. You can do anything you want." He responds, "No I can't, but if you can find a way that I can, I will be glad to."

He explains what he means by holding out his hand. He points to it as he holds it parallel to the ground and asks, "Have you ever seen a top without a bottom or a front without a back, or a day without a night? The same is with life. You can't appreciate happiness unless you have experienced unhappiness. You can't know pleasure unless you have been in pain. You can't understand success unless you have failed. It's a fact of life. Maybe it isn't the way you like it, but it is what makes you wise and strong and worthy of my reward." I think whoever wrote the screenplay for this film was right on with his or her insights as to the context of God and his world and our role in it.

The Kaballists believe Satan is God's divinely ordained partner who plays the role of the "heavy" in this divine drama of challenge between good and evil, right and wrong, pain and pleasure, success and failure and all the other many opposites that one must face and overcome in order to build the kind of life that reflects the quality that God hopes will be in all his children. It is this kind of common sense within the context of God's world and our place in it that I am trying to make understood within the pages of this book. I don't like pain but I have come to realize that I won't make any gains without overcoming it. I won't succeed unless I study. I won't know God unless I see his love in the crucified Jesus. Unless you can accept both sides of this contextual coin, you will walk with great frustration, pain and ignorance.

As Saint Paul said, "For now, we see through a mirror dimly. But one day, we will see face-to-face or clearly." (I Corinthians 13:12) Even though my understanding on this matter is dim, I too reach out like the little girl in the movie and wonder why it has to be this way. Well, God understands and in the context of his wisdom he has promised that one day, by my faith and through his grace, I will understand and be satisfied.

"In the beginning, God created the heavens and the earth." Many wise and knowledgeable people have tried to prove or challenge these words with human logic and scientific technology and, so far, haven't been able to verify their findings *beyond a shadow of a doubt* any more than those who believe them *by faith*. So, faith enters into the picture, as it always has, when people are confronted with unanswerable questions. It prompts us to contemplate that truth can be more important than fact. Personally, I find it impossible to comprehend creation, so I choose not to worry about it and get involved in that which is controversial. I accept by faith what the Bible says as well as what science contributes. I have spent my adult life focusing not on *how* this happened but on *what* should be done with it. It's more important, I think, to focus on living within creation than it is to understand how it came about.

It is not that I need to know the facts about creation as much as I need to know I will survive and make the best of the years in which I will live in what has been created. Commonsensible application of Biblical truth is more significant to me than mastering the scientific facts that I don't understand. Such facts are unnecessary for me. I trust in the knowledge of those who choose to make them the center of focus of their lives.

For me, the truth of the Bible within the context of its writers and its inspiration and applied within the context of my life is what holds my attention. As long as the facts aren't abused or used outside the biblical context I really don't care to know their details, no matter how interesting they may appear.

I need to concentrate on how to deal with people, places and events. I need wisdom to choose ways to make my life bear fruit, as Saint Francis says in his famous prayer, asking God to make him an "instrument of your (God's) peace; where there is hatred let me sow love; where there is doubt, faith; where there is despair, hope; where there is darkness, light and where there is sadness, joy. Let me not so much seek to be consoled as to console; not so much to be understood as to understand; not so much to be loved as to love . . ." Similarly, I pray that God will lead me not so much to seek to understand the nature of the world but to translate his nature into the hearts and minds of the world's inhabitants; not so much to know the facts of the creation as to serve the created; not so much to be smart as to be wise; not so much to succeed as to serve; not so much to accumulate facts as to do his will with what I have learned.

My life needs to produce the fruit of the Holy Spirit—love, joy, peace, patience, kindness, goodness, faithfulness, gentleness and long suffering (Galatians 5:22,23) rather than money, prestige, power and fame. I want to be a success, not only in *my* eyes but also in the mind and soul of the Being I believe created it all and who has a hope for me. How can I exist within the environment and with my fellow human beings? How can I put it all together within the context in which I find myself? I need knowledge and I need wisdom. Some is given. Some is natural, but much of it I must work hard to discover and understand for myself.

I didn't choose to live in this world, but I do choose to do something with my life now that I have been given it. I choose to take advantage of the abundant resources God has created and made available to me. I have his Word with its collection of inspired writings and relevant characters to help reveal knowledge and wisdom to me. I am blessed with people all around me, with whom I can share that which I believe God has revealed to me in his unique and wondrous way. I can also search the minds of great thinkers like Plato who said that some divinity has to be at the seat of creation. Isaac Newton said that a "divine intelligence" is responsible for all that we physically and mentally are capable of observing. Descartes said that he believed God created us simply because he found himself able to think. Blaise

Pascal, the great mathematician, calculated: "If I choose to believe in God my risk is finite and my possibilities infinite. If I choose to reject the existence of God, my gamble is infinite and my possibilities finite."

You don't have to be a Plato or a Newton or a Descartes or a Pascal to be knowledgeable. You do need to make use of their wisdom as well as that of Moses, David, the prophets or of Peter, Paul, John or James and certainly Jesus. You need to reveal yourself to others and to the Holy Spirit, whom Jesus promised will be with you to counsel and comfort you in your quest for truth and wisdom in the midst of your search for facts.

Wisdom is a gift, but it is worthless if it is not used to fulfill the will of God. Without faith in him; without hope in what he means to us; and without his love that generates it all, *all* the knowledge of *all* the facts about *all* the things within the universe will be in vain. James said, "Faith without works is dead." (James 2:17) Likewise knowledge without faith is futile. It is not how much you can know that counts; it's what you do with what you know.

Peter was probably an illiterate, but God gave him the gift of prophecy and wisdom so the big fisherman could catch souls. As a result you and I are forever seeking more knowledge within the context of the divine wisdom so we can love God, love each other and love ourselves. It is common sense within the context of faith that reminds us that Jesus said, "I am the Truth." (John 14:6)

EIGHTEEN

Victory at Lonesome Valley
Read: John 14:1-6 and 25-27

The title of this chapter and many of the sentiments expressed therein are inspired by an American folk hymn entitled "Jesus Walked This Lonesome Valley."

Jesus walked this lonesome valley. He had to walk it by Himself. O nobody else could walk it for Him. He had to walk it by Himself.

You must walk this lonesome valley. You need not walk it by yourself. For God sent His Son to walk it with us. We will not walk it by ourselves.

(Second stanza copyright 1976 by Fred Bock Music Co.)

Not long ago, a hero of mine died. She had contributed much to my professional capabilities and she didn't even know me. I became a better congregational pastor and hospital chaplain because of her words, the context from which they came and the context in which I applied them. She was a pioneer in the care of the sick, the suffering, the dying and their loved ones. She revolutionized the art of treating their spiritual needs. She enabled those who took her principles seriously to face that which is inevitable for each of us. Through her efforts and insights millions of dying people have walked through the lonesome valley of dying and death without the excess baggage of fear and anxiety. Her name was Elizabeth Kubler-Ross.

Two millennia ago my biggest and greatest hero died. He too contributed to the foundation of my ability to face dying and death, not only without fear and anxiety, but more importantly, with faith and hope. He showed me how to live and die. He didn't just author the words of eternal life; he was, is, and always will be the model, example, and guide for me, when I too experience the process of dying and the state of being dead. He is Jesus the Christ. He is, in my mind and heart, the Son of God and the Savior of my soul and the soul of anyone else who believes in him. It is his footprints that I see walking beside me as I walk through the valley and the shadow of death. When it all gets too difficult he carries me in his everlasting arms over the threshold and through the gates of paradise; that special state of being he has prepared for me and all who have trusted in the strength and common sense of his Gospel.

One of the greatest truths I have learned in my life is that God doesn't ask or expect me to do anything he wasn't or isn't first willing to do or be himself. Jesus walked this lonesome valley of death and that's why hundreds of millions of believers can and are willing to walk it with Him. He has promised to be at my side and to even pick me up when I falter on the way to heaven.

To many, the subject of dying and death is morbid and forbidding; one they would rather not think or talk about. Some of you might be a bit uncomfortable just reading about it. That is my point. Unless you are willing to face the issue; to listen to what God and his Word have to say about it and to observe Jesus honestly, as he walked the walk of death, death will remain a scary subject. Hundreds of years before Christ, Moses said that the strength or quality of life was the result of labor and sorrow, toil and trouble, hard work and personal discipline (Psalm 90:10). It was a revelation of God's universal principle of eternal growth and strength. It is when we reject running away from that which scares us and face life's obstacles that we defeat them and become strong enough for them to be powerless against us. If you are willing to face the tough things in life, then, when the final exam comes, you will attain the highest grade of God's precious words, "Well done, good and faithful servant." (Matthew 25:23)

Exercise your faith now and death will cease to be a barrier when you must walk through its valleys and shadows. If you choose to run away from the challenge of looking death in the eye now, you will not be strong enough nor have courage enough when it confronts you later. Death comes to each of us. How you face it will depend on your faith and how much you are willing to overcome the human tendency to run away from that which is difficult or threatening. Labor and sorrow, overcoming external obstacles and personal discipline are the keys to making death just another beautiful part of the Creator's divine plan of living. That keystone verse of Christianity, John 3:16, can be fulfilled in your life if you are willing to walk the path that leads to eternal life. Its memorable words say, "God so loved the world that He gave His only begotten Son, that whosoever believes in Him shall *not* perish but have everlasting life." God said it. I believe it.

Jesus walked this lonesome valley so you and I won't have to do so under a cloak of ignorance. What follows is my way of relating his act to our human context. He lived a human life and died a human death. It is God's way of saying, "I understand what you are going through. I've been there. I've done that." The Bible puts God into a human context and in simple commonsensible ways he reveals how he expects and hopes we will follow him into heaven. The Church has captured this frame of mind within the context of the Sacrament of Holy Communion. The suffering Savior seems to say, "I know pain and death and all that goes with it. I'm not asking you to do anything I wasn't first willing to do myself. Do this in remembrance of me." As a hospital and hospice chaplain I can attest to the value of this line of thinking. I have been able to help people face death by relating them to God through this simple, timeless, profound act of remembering him.

In her culture-shattering book, *On Death and Dying*, Elizabeth Kubler-Ross wrote that human beings move through five stages when they realize that they are going to die. They feel the pangs of denial, anger, bargaining, depression and acceptance. I strongly believe that Jesus also experienced these. It is important for me to know that the one person I trust more than any other to ensure my eternal well-being wasn't above going through that which he knows I too go through, too. That's what makes him so great and explains much of why his appeal is so universal. The Gospels graphically show that he understands the context of our lives and chose to help us navigate its storms with divine common sense and in the context of a life that is not much different from ours. It gives me courage, hope, and comfort to face whatever the future might bring in my last days. In Luke's Gospel (9:51) it says that there came a time in Jesus' life when "He turned His face toward Jerusalem." He acknowledged his inevitable death in a clear and forthright manner. I don't think there is much difference in this acknowledgement by Jesus and that of any of us, who hear the words of doom from a physician, when he realizes that his skills will not be able to stem the tide of a terminal illness.

After this definitive moment in his life, Jesus began His journey along the same road any human being must walk when it is his or her time to die. I am convinced that Jesus went through the typically human defense mechanisms that any of us have and will employ when we too face our finitude. He turned his thoughts away from death by getting involved in a running debate with the Scribes, Pharisees and Sadducees. He had to defend himself against their attacks on his claims and his revolutionary interpretation of how the Law and the Prophets must be fulfilled.

He immersed himself in mentoring the disciples and preparing them for the monumental task of giving birth to the Church and facing their enormous mission of helping her mature into the Body that has lasted to this very day. He didn't give himself a lot of time and opportunity to think about dying and death, and that fits perfectly the definition of the defense mechanism of "denial." I think it can also help one answer why he hesitated to run to the aid of Martha and Mary on the occasion of their brother Lazarus' death. It clearly shows that, no matter who you are and how great your faith may be, death is difficult to face.

From time to time during this period, he got angry. We read where he lost his temper in the Temple and drove out those who sold religious articles and sacrificial animals. He chastised those who took advantage of pilgrims to the Temple by cheating them when they had to exchange their secular money for Temple currency. (Matthew

21:12ff) He often verbally disciplined people. Just imagine how Peter felt when the Lord became angry with him for some of his mistakes and bad judgments. (Matthew 16:23) Then there was the time, just before his death, when he cursed a fig tree in a fit of temper. (Mark 11:20ff) Even on the cross, I think he angrily expressed his frustration at how his life was ending when he cried out passionately, "My God, My God, why have You forsaken Me?" (Matthew 27:46)

He even bargained with his heavenly Father. Just like any one of us who might wish to extend our lives for one reason or another, Jesus asked God if there might be some other way their divine plan could be accomplished. Three times in the Garden of Gethsemane, he asked his Father to somehow find a way to remove "this bitter cup" from him, each time quickly reaffirming that he knew that the timeless plan of redemption would be best and that God's will, not his, had to be done, no matter what the emotional, physical, or spiritual cost. (Mark 14:36)

Jesus became depressed during these days leading up to his final hour. Even his considerable spiritual energy was drained and he became fatigued. When he stood outside the tomb of his friend Lazarus, he wept. I believe that he realized that, in the not too distant future, he too would be entombed. (John 11) Again he wept when he stood at the crest of the hill outside Jerusalem on Palm Sunday. (Luke 19:41-44) Even with the crowd shouting "Welcome!" and "Hosanna," he wept, knowing that this would be one of the last times he would visit the city and before these same people would turn on him and shout, "Crucify him!"

And, of course, he accepted his fate. That's why he kept on keeping on after he had set his sights on Jerusalem. He talked openly of his fate as he walked toward the place in which he knew he would suffer, be humiliated and die. In the Garden, he faithfully yielded to his Father's will and said obediently, "Not my will by Thine be done." Then, on the Cross, he acknowledged the completion of his mission. (John 19:30) He gave up his spirit and committed it into the hands of his Father. (Luke 23:46) You too will experience this in some form or another. Will you be ready?

Keep your focus on this amazing person, Jesus Christ. Don't forget how he wanted us to think of him as a shepherd who promises that "you shall not want." He will make you lie down in peaceful pastures for spiritual nourishment with the fruits of his love, joy and peace. He defeated death in order to prove to you that he will fulfill his pledge to be patient, kind, good, faithful and gentle and to suffer your humanity. He will lead you beside still waters and take away your fear of the troubled waters of dying and death. He will restore your soul and show you the way of his peace.

Even when you walk through the valley and the shadow of death, you will need not fear because he promises to be with you. His rod and his staff —his word and his Spirit—will comfort you along the way. He will prepare a place for you in the midst of life's turmoil and even come again and receive you unto himself. With holy oil he will anoint your wounded life and a cup of blessing will be yours to overflowing. Surely goodness and mercy shall follow for all eternity and you will dwell in the house of God forever.

NINETEEN

What's On Your List?

Read: Deuteronomy 5:6-21 & 6:4-6; Micah 6:6-8; Matthew 5:3-12;
I Corinthians 12-13:13; and Galatians 5:22-23

Many a morning, at the breakfast table, my wife will ask, "What's on your list for today?" She knows I like to put on a three by five index card what I expect to accomplish in a day, or even more than a day. It is a discipline that helps me avoid surprises that might upset my equilibrium and hinder the accomplishment of my goals. Lists help me remember important basic information. They give me a foundation for what is on my mind and in my heart and soul. They help me organize my life and protect me from the many possibilities of chaos that can and often do occur. They reveal something about my obsessive-compulsive personality, which demands that I arrange my life in a way that manifests my Commonsensible Contextualism.

Lists are a shorthand tool that eliminates excess verbiage so I can concentrate on what is really important. If I can construct a good list, I will have provided myself a context of meaningful thoughts, principles, philosophies, theologies and factual knowledge. If I am to preach, teach and minister in God's name, I need to know as much of his will as possible so I can pass it on. Lists help me get started in fulfilling all that is required. They are an inventory of available information, which enables me to fill in some of the blanks of creative sermonizing. They are often the source of that which makes sense and creates the context upon which spiritual substance is built. Lists are my way of outlining my day, my thoughts, my dreams, my ministry, my sermons and my family obligations.

The Bible has many lists. Some are long and well known and have earned the respect of those who believe God is their author. Some are shorter but contribute significantly. From the Ten Commandments and the Beatitudes to the trilogies of Micah and Paul, there are lists that help you bring together a common-sense message that enables you to find the context in which God's plan will be fulfilled. Every day I say a prayer I read in a book by Glenn Clarke. It says, "I will to will the will of God!" It is a short list that puts my faith and hope into a context that is sensible, workable and reflects my personal will that I always pray will be in harmony with the will of God.

The biblical lists are magnificently designed by God to contribute to the redemption and sanctification of his human creatures. Some of them are obvious; some need to be investigated and analyzed, in order to discover the significance that may have been camouflaged with poetry and parable. Each is ordained by the Holy Spirit to give assistance in fulfilling the divine mission of revelation. The Christ came to assure abundant life through personal knowledge of God; knowledge that is so intimate that it conceives a new spiritual life, born from the union of the Holy Spirit and fertile human hearts, minds and souls.

The Ten Commandments are found in the fifth chapter of the Book of Deuteronomy. It is God's basic "do" list. In it he asserts his divine parental authority.

1. You shall have no other gods (power, prestige, pleasure, possessions, etc.) with greater importance or priority before me.

2. You shall not create within your mind or with your hands anything that might be worshipped as a substitute for or reproduction of me.

3. You shall not take me for granted or use my name in a meaningless, vain or thoughtless manner.

4. You shall hallow my name by setting aside a time for prayer, rest and worship.

5. You shall honor your parents, elders and mentors.

6. You shall not murder or degrade any human being.

7. You shall not break a holy commitment to me or your spouse or to anyone or anything with whom you have made a consecrated, personal obligation or contract.

8. You shall not steal.

9. You shall not lie.

10. You shall not crave anything that might become a god that would be greater in your esteem than me.

So many of these divinely inspired lists are usually considered to be linear in design. However, you need to see the subtle genius that makes the tenth Commandment become actually a lead in or return to the first, so when you contemplate the list, you find yourself in a circular process of behavior rather than one which has a beginning and an end.

Like a wedding band of gold, there is no actual beginning or end, just a divinely ordained behavioral process dedicated to giving glory to God through consecrated conduct. This design is a revelation from God to the discerning individual who is sensitive to the commonsensible message that is very often revealed through a context of literary design.

In the Torah, the first five books of the Hebrew testament, tradition says that God revealed through Moses a short list of how you should respect the Author of the Ten Commandments. The list is called the Shema. In Hebrew that means "hear." It can also be translated "listen" or "pay attention." Its full message is "God is One and you shall love Him with all of you your body, mind and spirit!"

(Deuteronomy 6:4,5) Jesus encouraged a Jewish lawyer to consider adding a passage from Leviticus (19:18b) as a commonsensible addendum: "You shall love your neighbor as yourself." (Luke 10:25) In true Christian fashion, he said that it was a fulfillment of Mosaic Law and a commonsensible contraction of what he considered to be the two greatest commandments of all.

From the writings that have become known as the New Testament, there is a short list that reveals the complete and divine nature of God. It is called the Trinity. In it, Yahweh is called Father, Son and Holy Ghost, meaning Creator, Redeemer and eternal, ever-present Counselor. The writers of these Holy Scriptures were inspired by God to project a divine mystery of one Being who is revealed through three personalities. It has been a source of faith and controversy, commonsensibly used by him to cause those who care to wrestle with his nature and not to take him for granted and use his name in vain. It is a great example of what I like to call the "Our Gang" method of moving a person from one place to another.

In the old Our Gang movies, the children had a dog they often tied to a wagon. They got him to pull it by dangling a hot dog on a string in front of his nose. As he chased (and never caught) the hot dog, he also pulled the wagon. I think God does the same to us; this Trinitarian mystery is a great example of getting us to think and wrestle with truth and to chase after it without end, thereby moving ourselves from one theological truth to another in a very commonsensible way and through several relevant and significant contexts.

Micah, one of the Minor Prophets, wrote a basic list of what God requires of us. (6:6-8) It is a little less definitive than the Ten Commandments. In it he is inspired by God to say that God wants you to *be* just, kind and humble. (Incidentally, this is what it means to be a prophet: to speak on behalf of someone else; in this case God.) The prophet presents a three-word list that conjures up many hours of prayerful thought. For example, the subject of justice can lead to some serious consideration of what the Golden Rule is all about. To me, it is the simplest definition of justice. To judge people as you want them to judge treat you is as fair as anything can be.

119

This golden gem of wisdom is to be found in every major world faith. Only in Christianity, though, is it expressed positively. Jesus said, "*Do* unto others what you would have them to *do* unto you." (Matthew 7:12) Other religions say the same thing but in a negative context: "*Don't do* what you *don't* want done . . ."

Micah says that God wants us to be kind. Jesus said that if we serve even the least of humanity with kindness, it is the same as serving him. (Matthew 25:39) To feed the hungry, clothe the naked, visit the sick or imprisoned, or even give a cup of cool water, in his name, to someone who is tired or stressed is a way of worshipping God. It is a way of fulfilling the oft-mentioned commandment to love God, love our neighbor and love ourselves. It is the simple manifestation of a commonsensible divine-human partnership within the context of everyday existence. Kindness doesn't require liturgy. All it calls for is common sense.

The prophet Micah says that God wants us to be just and kind in the context of humility. That's the Jesus way and truth of doing things. I think he would have approved the Nike athletic shoe company's motto: "Just do it!" In many places, the Bible repeats God's simple commonsensible admonition, "If you love me, keep my commandments" I think he is saying "Don't take me for granted. Love me with all of your body, mind and spirit. Be fair in your behavior, be kind to others and do so in a manner in which you show your humble acceptance of my common sense within the context of your life and my world."

Speaking of behavior, I would be remiss if I didn't mention Jesus' famous list of rules for Christian *be-havior*. I speak, of course, of the *Be-Attitudes*. That's the way Robert Schuller once described them. It is a list of attitudes or actions that identify you as a Christian. It is a directory, if you will, of the attributes of those who have found holiness, happiness or blessedness in Jesus Christ. It says that happy Christians are those who are *poor in spirit*; those who acknowledge their sinful indebtedness to God. It reveals that by his grace, the debt is forgiven because they are willing to sacrifice their most cherished possession, their ego. Then he says that a comforted Christian is one who *mourns* for his or her sin; is *meek* (tames the ego, is obedient*)*; *hungers and thirsts after righteousness* like a starving person longs for food or one who is dying of thirst craves water.

He concludes this monumental list from the Sermon on the Mount by saying that those who are *merciful* will be blessed by God's mercy; those who are *pure in heart* will understand him, those who *make peace* will become children of God by being brothers and sisters of Christ; and those who are willing to be *persecuted* (vulnerable) *for righteousness* (for his sake) will be rewarded with residency in heaven. I will go into a more extensive discussion of this cornerstone of Christian living in the next chapter.

In I Corinthians 13:13, Saint Paul gives a list of three things that will energize the Beatitudes or any other effort to obey, worship or serve God. They are *faith, hope* and *love* and they are the fuel that gives power to the believer so he or she can fulfill the "*Do*" of the Ten Commandments or the "*Be*" of the Beatitudes.

The Apostle to the Gentiles also gives two other lists that are part of the foundation for his architectural blueprint for what has become the Christian Church. In them he tells of God's special gifts that are bestowed through the presence and baptism of his Holy Spirit that Jesus promised to his disciples in the Upper Room. These gifts of the Holy Spirit can be briefly listed as *wisdom, knowledge, healing, miracles, prophecy, discernment, tongues* and *the interpretation of ecstatic tongues.* Paul goes into detail about these in I Corinthians 12 and 14, which are interestingly separated by the 13th or "Love Chapter." Through these gifts, God is able to mobilize individuals and enable the Church to minister effectively and, in spite of its human frailties, to prosper and succeed in fulfilling Christ's mission. In this list you will find a wealth of resources that are available if you are willing to do what it takes to recognize them and accept them. If you do, God will bless you with the gift of a cornucopia of fruit that befits his appreciation of your faith in him and your acceptance of the wisdom I have listed above.

In his letter to the Galatians (5:22-23), Paul gave another list of God's fruitful rewards for the faithful believer. In it he said that such a person would experience *love, joy* and *peace*, along with his *patience, kindness, goodness, faithfulness, gentleness* and *long suffering.*

Lists are much more than their words. The whole of them is often greater than their obvious parts. Better yet, when you are able to check off each item as fulfilled or accomplished, you will move one step closer to intimately knowing God and his Christ; one step closer to heaven; one step closer to eternal life; one step closer to being "filled full."

Before I end this chapter, I want to add one more list for your consideration. It isn't a list that you will find in the Bible. It isn't the result of Christian thought. It wasn't penned by a Christian. It was written by someone who lived six centuries before Jesus. I present for your contemplation a list that I believe God has revealed to the world through the ancient philosopher Siddhartha Gautama, better known as the Buddha, "the awakened one." I'm sure many of you might think it improper of me to include this non-Christian person's thoughts to be considered in the same vein as that of the Lord Jesus Christ or the revered Moses or the venerable Saint Paul or any of the saintly prophets.

Let me explain my reason for including the thoughts of this great historical and philosophical (not religious) personage. Buddhism is technically not a religion. It falls more in the realm of philosophy than theology. However, it is so close that scholars and thinkers have wrestled with how to categorize it for more than two millennia. Personally, I find that which the Buddha has to say is at times very compatible with the way and the truth of Jesus.

It makes sense to me that God in his wisdom has found a way to reveal his truth and way to many cultures at different times through a variety of people. I know there will be some that will think less of me for equating Gautama's words with those believed to be divinely inspired in the only true source of divine truth, the Bible. I don't presume to equate Buddha's words with those of the Bible. I choose to use them to make the message of the Bible more commonsensible. I take literally the best known passage of the Gospels as my prompt to do what I have done: "God so loved the *world* . . ." (John3:16) Why not use some of the wisdom of the world to modify and enhance biblical truth? Somehow, I believe the hand of God is involved in both.

In my old age, I take seriously the admonition: "To thine own self be true." I am convinced God gave me a brain and common sense as well as a faith in his divine revelation. He had endowed me with freedom to use them to work out my salvation in partnership with his Holy Spirit. I seek not to take him for granted or in vain. I seek not to place my beliefs before his or create from within my mind that which would be substituted for what I have discovered to be his true word. I seek truth within the context of commonsensible faith. And I believe that what I am to say is inspired by the Holy Spirit as much as the words of Moses or the prophets or David of Paul or Peter or many other great Christians.

You be the judge. I feel called to write what I think will give you something with which to wrestle for yourself what God wants to be your personal foundation of faith and eternal life. Like Jacob, I believe God will change you and bring you to a relationship that transcends words. You will become more than your thoughts, beliefs, and religion; more than the sum of your parts.

First let me share with you the Four Pillars on which Buddhism is built:

1. Life is *dakkah* (Sanskrit for dislocation or separation).

2. Dakkah is caused by *tanha* (craving, lust, covetousness, egoism)

3. Nirvana is the state in which dakkah is eliminated.

4. The Eightfold Path is the "way" to arrive at Nirvana (heaven?; the place of perfect peace)

    a.   Right views (*understanding*)

    b.   Right thoughts (*wrestling*)

    c.   Right speech (*communication, expression*)

    d.   Right conduct (*action*)

    e.   Right livelihood (*lifestyle*)

    f.   Right effort (*discipline*)

    g.   Right mindfulness (*Be-attitude?*)

    h.   Right concentration (*focus*)

(Italics and oversimplifications mine)

I believe that in many ways this list is in harmony with many Christian principles. I approach it not as scripture but as a means by which I can broaden my understanding of Holy Writ and Christian doctrine. Think about it; wasn't the problem of Adam and Eve one of craving for the fruit of the Tree of the Knowledge of Good and Evil? Weren't they tempted by Satan to equate themselves with God? Did not God "dislocate" them from the paradise of Eden because of their rebellion and egoism? I then ask myself, did not God send his Son to be the expiation for this alienation, dislocation and separation from paradise, and did not his Son tell us that eternal restoration of this state of dislocation will come by "intimately knowing God?" (John 17:3) Therefore, I ask, does not such knowledge come through human understanding, and understanding by thinking, and thinking by speaking with others who might share their wisdom? Does not the person of faith come to a knowledge of God by faithful action? Saint James said, "Faith without works is dead." (James 2:26)

Therefore, is it not common sense to say that understanding without action is dead? Is it unreasonable to agree that such action leads to a lifestyle that is developed by right effort, right attitude and right focus? One of my favorite hymns says, "Turn your eyes upon Jesus. Look full in his wonderful face." By focusing on the supreme righteousness of Jesus Christ and creating an attitude of faith, I believe I will, in time, cease to be dislocated by sin and be restored to reside eternally in his presence. I believe the principles of the Buddha are not contrary to those of Jesus but actually assist me in knowing him better. I think they are worth considering. I don't base my salvation on the Buddah or his philosophy but I do find his principles helpful in understanding my Christian self. Then again, that's the way I see it. I wonder, how do *you* see it?

Didn't God reveal the Ten Commandments and the Beatitudes as signposts for our journey to heaven? I think the Buddha's wisdom says that the person who walks the Eightfold Path will hunger and thirst after a right understanding of *the* right "knowledge" through right thoughts, right fellowship, right behavior, right labor and right sorrow. He or she will be someone whose righteous attitude will be one of love for God, neighbor and self and will be someone who is totally focused by faith in God as he reveals himself through the grace of Jesus Christ. The philosophy of the Buddha has helped me deepen my insight of the Christian path which leads me to a hungering and thirsting for the Way and the Truth and the Life that is Jesus Christ.

I find these thoughts to be in harmony with the eightfold pathway of Jesus' Beatitudes. I can hear my Lord say to me, as he did to that young Pharisaic lawyer who wanted to know which were the greatest commandments, "Do this and you will live!" It is the common sense of Buddha within the context of Jesus Christ.

TWENTY

Infinite Wisdom
Read: Matthew 5:1-10

Imagination is a blessed gift from God. Using it creatively you can wrestle with the words of the Bible and discover the wisdom and understanding that can be found within the context of its common sense and divine revelation. Sometimes I think television has robbed us of our imagination's great value. I remember the days of my youth when I would listen to radio drama and have to create the scene of the action within the limits of my "mind's eye." It occurs to me that I'm a slow reader because of this. I take a lot of time to create scenes in my mind that are suggested by an author's descriptions. To make the point of this chapter I choose to have you use your imagination to penetrate the depths of the infinite wisdom of Jesus' Beatitudes.

In your mind's eye, imagine a circle where the number 1 is at the top where 12 would be on a clock and 8 where 11 would normally be on that clock. My purpose is to have you conclude that the Beatitudes are of infinite wisdom. Like the Ten Commandments, I believe they are not linear but circular and never ending. When the eighth Beatitude is absorbed you find yourself starting all over again with the first, and on and on to infinity. The wisdom of Jesus like that which God inspired Moses to copy on tablets of stone can never come to and end. It is forever being renewed in the mind, heart and soul of a believer.

This symbol I am suggesting for you to create within your imagination could be considered to be a form of idolatry, like the images the second Commandment forbids. Idols can be mental and spiritual as well as materials such as stone, wood or metal. The prohibition against graven images (statuary) is just as relevant to that which your mind and imagination can also create as substitutes for God. Jesus told a Samaritan woman that God is Spirit and the time was at hand when true worshipers would worship him in "Spirit and in Truth."

There are those who interpret symbols as being sinful "graven images." To others they are alternative means of expressing divine truth. Once again I am persuaded that the context goes a long way in determining if a symbol is to be called a sin or not. Some people define sin as doing bad things. I like to characterize it as the abuse of that which is good. Therefore if one idolizes a symbol (a cross, communion host, statue, icon, even music and suggestions like that which I have made above) then it is a sin, but if that symbol is a means to the end of strengthening one's faith, then I believe it is perfectly within the bounds of proper conduct and belief. It seems to me that, within the boundaries of this subject, at least, sin is in the eye of the beholder. There are those whose worship practices are wrapped up in liturgy, statuary, iconography and other physical representations of spiritual truths and those who find any material representation of anything that might in any way be worshipped or revered to be anathema. It all depends on whose eye is beholding the objects and what their faith group has determined what proper belief and behavior will be.

Previously I used the symbol of the triangle and the tree to clarify or illustrate some of the things I believe. In this instance I choose to use an imaginary symbol of a circle to represent what I find to be the common sense of the Beatitudes of Jesus within the context of my world and his. The circle can be a focal point on which you can give meaning to the eight steps Jesus suggests a believer is blessed or made happy, fulfilled, satisfied or saved by.

If you choose to read this classic sermon outline as a list, I think you may not realize the full benefit of its infinite wisdom. As a list, the Beatitudes is a wonderful way to learn the sacred principles Jesus chose to present in common-sense terms. But put it into the context of the symbol for perpetuity and you are able to see a much broader lesson with greater personal consequences.

As usual, the Master has found a way to append multiple truths to each statement. There is an obvious truth and at least one more subtle gem. That is the genius of the entire Bible. God has used the minds of human beings to reveal his Truth and he does it in such a way as to appeal to the variety of personalities within the many eras of human history and within the contexts of many cultures. Like the aforementioned time-release capsules, these truths come to mind at different times, brought on by a multitude of stimuli in order to accomplish his will and enlighten his children within their individual context of time, place, culture, tradition, and religion.

With this in mind, let us proceed to follow the track of divine wisdom as presented by Jesus on that hill in Palestine to the ears and minds of first-century Jews. Let us marvel at how God can bring truth to our understanding in the twenty-first century in the same way he could in the first and not need to change a word in the process.

The first symbol to be noted is that Jesus assumed a sitting position. This was the way of the rabbis. When a rabbi, teacher, or master sat down, he symbolically told those who chose to listen that what he was saying was to be understood as worth hearing, remembering and putting into practice. In today's world, a teacher, preacher or rabbi stands and the congregation sits. In Jesus' day, it was the reverse. What the Lord is telling us at the very outset of the Sermon on the Mount is: "This is important. Listen carefully. I have thought this through and what I am about to say is the truth, the whole truth and nothing but the truth!"

He then proceeds to list eight attitudes that will reflect the inner faith of a believer. They are eight keys to eternal happiness. They do not stand alone, although they could; they complement each other and they flow like a circle neverending within the context of his day and ours.

First comes "Blessed are the poor in spirit, for theirs is the Kingdom of Heaven." The key to understanding Jesus' intent with this statement is what the term "poor in spirit" symbolizes or represents. On the surface it can be taken as referring to one's bank account or material wealth. It wasn't unusual for Jesus to take the side of the poor on economic issues, but not in this case. Poverty of spirit, in this instance, is one's spiritual value and he is beginning his list with that which would establish a proper relationship between a human and God. God is God and humans are humans and when they realize and accept this then they are free to proceed and know that the ultimate universal Being loves even the "least of his human creatures" and that he will designate them as his heirs to a kingdom that is above and beyond the earth and all material creation and to fix their tenure as residents within it as being eternal.

The question arises, "What must I do to achieve this poverty of spirit? The answer is simple, but the practice is difficult and without the grace of God it cannot be achieved by human effort. Sacrifice and humility are the keys that open the door to a broad context of interpretation, from the one extreme of those who would adopt an ascetic stance to those who would choose to give up some personal bad habit, from those who would intentionally mutilate their body to glorify God and demean themselves, to those who would give up chocolate for Lent. Personal sacrifice for the good of solidifying one's relationship with God can obviously be achieved in as many ways as there are people to attempt to fulfill this "attitude of being."

Later in Matthew's Gospel (16:24), Jesus would sharpen his definition of how to attain blessed poverty of spirit. He said, "If any one would accept me and my Way, then let him take up his cross and follow my lead, walk in my footsteps." Little did those who were to hear these words the first time understand how much the Cross would come to represent and symbolize his truth. How much more do those of us in the twenty-first century realize that laying down one's life (sacrifice one's ego, if you will) in service to Christ would be the ultimate gesture of devotion, faith and acceptance? And the reward would be to be designated an heir to the wealth of eternal life within a kingdom prepared by God for those who "know" him (John 17:3).

The second Beatitude is less difficult to interpret: "Blessed are those who mourn, for they shall be comforted." If you can avoid being drawn into the most frequently used meaning for the term *to mourn,* you will discover another treasure of divine truth in what I find often to be a misinterpretation of the Lord's meaning. Instead of the kind of mourning one does when someone near and dear dies, it is quite conceivable that Jesus was talking about the kind of emotional and spiritual discomfort that is involved in an act of personal discipline; the kind he experienced during those forty days and forty nights in the wilderness preparing for his ministry and his hour of trial; the kind of "labor and sorrow" that Moses experienced on Mount Sinai; the kind of discipline Noah and his family experienced. (The number forty is often used in scripture as a literary tool to denote a long period or time of personal discipline.)

It is not unusual for the words "No pain, no gain" to be painted on the walls of a gym or locker room. This paraphrase of the words of Psalm 90:10 says very well what Jesus meant when he urged the believer to have an attitude of sacrifice and discipline in order to attain the blessed state of realizing that forgiveness awaits those who mourn for their sin and repent from the ways that separate a soul from God. The road to forgiveness and eternal spiritual comfort begins with the difficult first step of acknowledging one's sin and working hard to overcome it through the pain of submitting the ego to the rigors of penance. It isn't a paradox to say, "Happy is the person who mourns." It is the formula for forgiveness. Hard work and personal discipline is God's universal principle of strength and spiritual quality. Psalm 90:10 says that we may live to be seventy or eighty years old but the strength or quality of life comes in labor and sorrow, hard work and personal discipline.

Another easy to misinterpret Beatitude is the third. "Blessed are the meek" is too often misconstrued to mean blessed are those who submit rather than stand up to a challenge or defend a principle; someone who runs away from a threatening situation or cowers in the presence of unsavory opposition. "Casper Milquetoast" is the most common description for someone who is meek. That's *not* what it means. It is one of those positive words that have been changed into a negative by the evolution of language. I stand by the word's original meaning of "quiet strength." I once heard meekness defined as the act of "taming the ego." To me that falls right into harmony with the intent of Jesus' first two attitudes of Christian faith and behavior. To sacrifice one's self and ego is to invest in the poverty of spirit that produces the riches of the Kingdom of Heaven. To mourn for one's sin and grow strong through personal discipline produces a person who is sturdy enough to tame the ego and to stand tall and not have to justify him—or herself in the light of the wisdom and folly of the world.

The informed Christian will readily observe that Jesus lived within the context of his words. He practiced what he preached. He expects those who follow him to apply his teaching within the context of their lives. Without question he obeyed his Father's plan. With firm resolution he did what he had to do and, I believe with all that is sacred within me, he did it well!

The fourth Beatitude brings the believer to the summit of the Sermon on the Mount. Sacrifice, penance, discipline and hard work have produced the strength that has enabled the serious disciple to achieve his or her highest goals. In this case Jesus uses these truths to propel the believer to the highest point of life; the one in which the person is totally and completely righteous. Is it not the goal of a Christian to do that which is right in the sight of God? I often pray a prayer I learned from the writer Glenn Clarke. He said, "I will to will the will of God." I have paraphrased that prayer into one of my own: "I know that I know that I want to know God."

To be righteous is to know God. Jesus defined eternal life as knowing God (John 17:3). The product of my personal discipline is being strong enough to do what is right in the sight of God. It is also that which will enable me to launch into the downhill portion of this mountaintop experience; to act like a Christian by being willing to be merciful, peacemaking, pure and vulnerable. In short, to be like

Jesus Christ, I have discovered that his way is the greatest road map on the highway of life; a path that leads to heaven. It is the key to what he promised his disciples when he told them in the Upper Room that he would prepare a place for those who believe and practice the Beatitudes.

Hungering and thirsting will be rewarded by the satisfaction of being filled with the most nourishing and delicious spiritual food ever fashioned by the Creator of the universe. As a feast of fine food produces a contentment of satisfied tastes and is filling, so the blessing of the feast of righteousness will satisfy those who consume and digest the word of God through Jesus Christ. When the Bread of Heaven nourishes the soul and blood of the Lamb and the wine of salvation titillates the spirit, the believer will understand what it will mean to enjoy the Marriage Supper of the Lamb that is prophesied in the Book of Revelation (19:9). The view from the top is worth it. In the Beatitudes it is a preview of the coming paradise of heaven for those who know God and who have learned to know him through Jesus Christ.

Beatitude five makes sense. "Blessed are the merciful, for they shall obtain mercy." It is in harmony with Jesus' later teaching in his prayer, which says in part, "forgive us our debts as we forgive our debtors." This is cause and effect that is almost impossible to miss. It only makes sense to assume that even if the world takes advantage of the person who is merciful, God will reward him or her with the mercy that he speaks of in the above mentioned disciplines. The person who is strong enough to follow the lead of Jesus and show mercy will reap the benefits that Jesus reaped, even though the world rejected and crucified him.

Mercy will come to those who resist the temptation to satisfy "number one"—themselves. Follow the lead of Jesus and endure the world and the consequences will be worth your faithfulness. Be faithful to the Christian principle of meekness and be comforted in the face of being misunderstood. Hunger and thirst after righteous mercy and you will experience the satisfaction of being filled full of the expectations of Christ for those who follow him. Sacrifice self and be blessed with the mercy of forgiveness and the riches of inheriting the Kingdom of Heaven. Those who love and wish to worship God will do so by being merciful. Jesus said in the parable of the sheep and the goats (Matthew 25 31ff), "When you do something merciful unto even the least of His brethren (all God's children,) it's the same as doing it unto Him."

Next the Lord says that people with pure hearts will see God. I want to make sure you realize something I think you already know. It is the awareness that a good synonym for "see" is "understand." The Buddha was blessed by God to comprehend this gem of wisdom. In his Eightfold Path, the founder of one of the world's greatest and most enduring religions/philosophies said that the destination of life's pathway to heaven is understanding. He says that right understanding is the result of right thoughts, right conversation with others who deepen your insights, right actions, right lifestyle, right effort, right attitude and right focus. It is interesting to me that God would see fit to complement his revelation through Jesus with thoughts and principles of the Buddha. I realize that some would call this an error in judgment, maybe even heresy. Yet the common sense of the context of the lives of these two great people and me seem to be in harmony and reflect the intent of the divine Truth.

To see God is to know him intimately. Understanding the mysteries of the Bible by the power of the Holy Spirit (his rod and his staff) will enlighten and comfort the believer in the presence of the enemy of sin. It will transcend cerebral knowledge and reveal the realm of intimacy which conceives a new being who is born again into a new and everlasting existence. God has prepared a table of blessing in the midst of the one who even tempted Jesus so we might see him and find the way and the truth that leads to eternal life. Pure thoughts come from those who have disciplined themselves to resist the impurities that the world thinks are acceptable. They come from the hearts of those who are willing to sacrifice the pleasures of the material and the immoral world that is so prevalent today and who are hungry and thirsty for that which is right.

As I write these words it is the season of the year in which I am preparing for the celebration of the birth of the Prince of Peace—certainly an appropriate title for Jesus. If he was anything, he was a man who espoused peace and laid down his life within the context of violence to obtain it for all who believe in him and cast their faith on who he was, what he did and why he did it. It isn't surprising that he would call "blessed" those who would be peacemakers. He goes so far as to promise an equal portion of his divine inheritance with anyone who is willing to believe in him. I know I'm admonished not to make changes to the Word of God, but I find some truth in a thought that came to me some years ago when I was in the midst of counseling a particularly difficult domestic squabble. It came to me that Jesus practiced what he preached and when he said, "Blessed are the peacemakers, for they shall be called the sons of God," he could just as easily have said, "Blessed are the peacemakers, for they shall be caught in the middle." It isn't unusual for someone who is attempting to bring two disputing parties together into a restored and harmonious relationship to become caught in the middle and end up feeling the arrows of their hatred. Jesus lived this phenomenon. When the Son of God laid down his life to take away the sins of those who rebelled against God, He found himself literally hanging between heaven and earth, between God and mankind. And because he was faithful to his Father's plan, he was blessed with resurrection and the complete fulfillment of that plan. He was comfortable in promising to those who follow him the title of "Son of God." I like the old proverb: "The Son of God became a Son of Man so the sons of men could become the sons of God."

If I were to ask most anyone what they desire most in life, I am confident they would reply, "Peace—peace of mind, body, and spirit, domestic tranquility, neighborhood harmony, national and international peace." More than wealth and possessions, the human spirit covets peace. Without it, all else is meaningless or worthless. The peace which Christ promises to his followers is beyond their understanding. It is something they long for with a passion reserved for nothing else. Blessed are those who strive to bring this treasure to others. As I said above, if you give it to others, it's the same as giving it to God and what greater offering can any one of us present to God than peace on earth and goodwill among its residents?

I'm aware that Jesus once said that he did not come to bring peace, but a sword that would divide people. That was within a context that is overshadowed by a contrary idea. He endured violence so you and I could find the peace that passes understanding. Sometimes you have to make a point by saying something outrageous. In the midst of my life's turmoil I have always been blessed with the knowledge and belief that through it all awaited me this indescribable peace from this incomparable Person. I am blessed because the ultimate Peacemaker practiced exactly what he preached and was willing to go through hell so I might reside in heaven. Blessed is he who came in the name of the Lord and blessed are his feet which have brought these good tidings. (Nahum 1:15)

With the eighth Beatitude we are brought back to the threshold of the first. This one testifies that those who are willing to be persecuted for righteousness' sake will possess the Kingdom of Heaven. My grandfather used to tell me that if anything was worth having, it was worth working for. Many a patriot has proclaimed that freedom and peace are worth dying for. So too says Jesus. Those who are willing to be vulnerable to the powers of the world will be blessed with ownership of an eternal residence in the presence of God himself.

Saint Paul said that God was, in Christ, reconciling himself to the world. In like thought, he also took on the limitations of human nature and put himself in jeopardy by confronting Satan. God was, in Christ, vulnerable in the wilderness, in the garden and on the cross and probably, in many ways, every day of his life. I don't think God ever asks us to do or be anything he isn't first willing to do himself. God came into this world in a way beyond the comprehension of mortal minds to save us from ourselves. He gave himself the freedom of choice that you and I possess and succeeded in defeating the temptations and influences that have defeated us and damned us. By his grace and courage, he accepted the vulnerability of human nature so that Satan would lose dominion over God's most precious creatures.

Those who would walk in the steps of the Master must also be willing to take up a cross or lay down their lives, egos and personal agendas. The reward is the blessings we have been discussing in this chapter. If you would be saved from sin and those instincts that would separate you from God, then you need to be willing to walk through hell for a heavenly cause, to look Satan in the eye and hold firmly to the spirit of Jesus, who walked the walk rather than merely talking the talk. Greater love has no one than to be vulnerable enough to sacrifice his body and soul for God. The blessings of Christ are to those who take his Beatitude seriously and walk its walk, because when it becomes impossible, the Christ will cease to walk beside you and take you in his arms and carry you over the troubled waters of life and death and into the peace of heaven.

When you complete this Beatitude and look up you will find yourself starting all over again with the first of the Christ's eightfold blessed attitudes. You will be better prepared to accept and glory in your poverty of spirit and keep the journey alive to infinity.

CONCLUSION?

As I bring this book to a conclusion, I am drawn to the realization that it has come to symbolize several things to me. It is, hopefully, a legacy for my children and grandchildren, a testimony of what has come to be, for me, a journey of incredible growth and discovery and a discipline of spiritual fulfillment and understanding. Other sacred writings have caught my attention and crossed my path from time to time. Unexpected sources like strangers, friends, patients or parishioners, experiences and especially the Holy Spirit, in his own subtle ways, has helped me chart a course that I have come to believe he plotted before I was born. As I said earlier, I have often considered all these influences to be like time-release capsules. Some truths were immediately evident, others took time to materialize and still others appeared late in my life, when common sense and context seemed to release their impact in a special way.

I'm sure you have noted the many repetitious references that have appeared in this collection of what were at one time sermons. They indicate not only a consistency in my thinking and development but also a realization that a few simple gems of wisdom and divine truth can build a personal theology, sustain a faith and motivate a life. Add to this, the works of scholars in religion, philosophy, psychology and God's Word and you will discover the foundation that I KNOW has and will continue to sustain my soul as I overcome the resistances of the world and/or Satan. I have no doubt that one day I will have proved strong enough to endure this life and then stand before my God with confidence in his grace and hope in my faith. The simple truths around which I have written this book are all I have needed to get me to where I am ready, willing and able to take the last breath of this life and gasp the first in the next.

At first, I wrote for my own discipline and personal needs. It ended up with a hope that my children and grandchildren will capture some of the faith I have found and the love I have for God. What it might mean to anyone else who is willing to read it will be up to them and the God who inspired me to write it. This has been an exercise in faith by a man who is flawed. It isn't expected to have been a literary masterpiece. A mentor once told me that I write like a preacher. If it is ever published, I will be surprised. I believe God will have to move some mountains of literary inadequacy and overcome much of my theological weakness if anyone beyond those for whom I will print a few copies will appreciate it enough to read it, let alone publish it.

Life is a journey and its final destination is reached by following a divine map that has been laid out for me by sources I sincerely believe have been sent by God. It's that map on which I would like to draw this labor of love to a Commonsensible Contextual conclusion. I haven't always followed it as I should and many times I didn't stop to ask directions. It is always there and available—and accurate. The landscape of my life has been laid out like an atlas so I have assigned numbers to the various routes. Each has a purpose and a destination which I believe God wants me to find. As with the preceding chapters, please bear with me and allow the Holy Spirit's thoughts to flow through my fingers and onto the page. In the spirit of Commonsensible Contextualism, let me once more challenge you to think about the highways and byways that have helped me, and just maybe will help you, to know God.

The main highway on my system I call "The Big Purple One." It honors my God, the King of Kings. He is Allah, THE God. He is Yahweh, I AM. His name is not to be taken in vain as certainly as he can never be taken for granted. He is the definitive *one* in all of creation, the "Numero Uno" before whom is no other. Some say there is only one God. I don't. I recognize thousands of gods who vie for my attention and adoration. None of them can ever challenge the unbounded glory of Yahweh Allah. None can be compared and measured the same as he because he is beyond measurement and beyond description.

The message of Highway no. 1 is simple: God is above all other deities such as power, prestige, money and pleasure. They tempt me to bow down to that which would give me pleasure and self-gratification. He appeals to my desire to know him and to serve him by serving others. That ever-present god, the ego, too often gets higher priority than Yahweh. That cannot be. God and God alone is number one, all the rest fall into line far away from his glory. They can never come close to the OMNIpotent, the OMNIscient, and the OMNIpresent God of gods. The Big Purple One is the one that leads me to the royal mile in that Kingdom which shall have no end.

Going in the same direction as Route no. 1 is a secondary street I call Bill Cosby Avenue. As I contemplate its significance, I am reminded that although I am created in the image of God, I am limited by my nature to be equal with him. I came to this name because of a comedy skit Bill Cosby recorded many years ago. In it God and Noah have a dialogue. At the end, the old man is exasperated at all that the Lord has demanded of him. He can't see a purpose for it all. He is stressed out because his neighbors ridicule him. The mess in the bottom of the boat is causing him much discomfort. When he has just about reached his limit of endurance and patience, he hears thunder in the distance and the rain begins to fall with ever-increasing volume. He soon pauses and humbly turns to his God and simply says "Okay, God, you and me." That's the point of Route no. 2. He is God. I am man. He is number one. I am number two. Later there will be an acknowledgement of the two of us being united in another magnificent street inside the Kingdom of God. We will testify to our completeness when, by his grace and my faith, we are intimately united forever.

The third highway on my map is called "The Trilogy Trail." It is my way of bringing into my scheme of meditation the trilogies that I presented for your consideration in chapter 6. A trip on this highway helps me focus on such things as God's name, his nature, the energy necessary to believe and follow him and the requirements he makes of us. When I spend time on the Trilogy Trail, I find greater intimacy with Jesus because he is, for me, the Way, the Truth and the Llife. With him I find the serenity to accept the things I cannot change, the courage to change the things I can and the wisdom to know the difference. It helps me see him more clearly, love him more dearly, and follow him more nearly, day by day.

I call Highway no. 4 "Humana Highway." This is a way for me to strengthen my realization that I am finite and that, as a human being, my earthly existence is limited to the four points of the compass—north, east, south and west—and that I live within the physical environment of the seasons—spring, summer, winter and fall. I can put this into a humanly spiritual context that I am to respond to God with my heart (passion), mind (intellect), soul (spirit) and strength (body) so I can learn of him, serve him and hallow his name.

The "Torah Turnpike" is the name I give to my Route no. 5. It is the address for the law firm of Genesis, Exodus, Leviticus, Numbers and Deuteronomy. In this seminal part of the Hebrew Testament, God reveals to mankind that from his mind the universe was conceived. It presents the labor and delivery of a people of faith and records his role as divine parent. His rules for human behavior and the establishment of dynamics for family life are revealed in the stories of Adam and Eve, Abraham and Sarah and their descendants, as well as Moses and the recalcitrant Children of Israel.

I call Route no. 6 the "Garden Path." It is a dead-end street filled with potholes. It also runs alongside a slippery slope that ends up in chaos after winding through the tempting foothills of gluttony, lust, greed and pride on the way to nowhere on Ego Mountain. It was designed and built by Satan and traveled by all of us, including the Lord Jesus. As I travel this road, I wrestle with my own personal theory that Satan isn't some diabolical fiend who would destroy God, but is his faithful servant whose responsibility is to force me to overcome any and all of the obstacles he can devise to make me a worthy citizen of heaven. I know that my hypothesis is not widely accepted and is constructed on a shaky foundation, but I find much insight into God's grace when I match Psalm 90:10 (the strength of life is labor and sorrow) with the story of Job and that of Jesus' temptation in the wilderness.

It's stuff like this that I want to submit for your consideration. I want you to be like Jacob and wrestle with your God. I strongly believe that if you do, he will bless you just as he blessed Jacob on the fateful night along the River Jabbok. It is just something which has danced through my mind for a long time. God will correct me if I'm wrong. So far, I feel pretty comfortable. Do me a favor and think about it. He who wrestles with God will be blessed. I wouldn't lead you down the garden path of destruction. I would make you work for your blessings. Anything worth possessing is worth working for.

Highway no. 7 I call "Complete Street." The Bible was written in the part of the world called the Middle East. Numbers carry great symbolic meaning there. When the divine "3" and the human "4" come together they add up to the complete "7." That symbolizes the goal God has always had for this world and for us. He is completed when you and he come together and intimately know each other. This is true in reverse as well; you and I are complete when we come together with God and are born again. I mentioned earlier that one street would be the fulfillment of my daily prayer: "Okay, God, you and me!" On Complete Street, I feel the presence of God fulfilling me in ways far beyond what I deserve. On this street both of us reside and live together in mutual love, respect and complete fulfillment.

I have a dual expressway on my map. I call it Route no. 88, "The Sonshine Highway." It offers me the opportunity to relate the eight Beatitudes of Jesus with the Eightfold Pathway of the Buddha. Winding side by side, they lead me on a meditative highway to the gates of heaven/nirvana where it becomes Route no. 9, "The Golden Mile"—the main street of heaven that isn't paved with gold but with the fruits of the Holy Spirit that God revealed through Saint Paul in Galatians 5.

The pavement of the Golden Mile is love, joy and peace. But before you can ride on this grand thoroughfare, a toll must be paid. The blood of the Lamb of God is its payment and the other six gifts of his Spirit serve as the currency with which it is paid: patience, kindness, goodness, faithfulness, gentleness and long suffering. Once again the blessed truth of all of this happens by his grace, through your faith.

The final road on my map I call "The Ten-C Beltway." It circles my imaginary kingdom and gives discipline to my life. Doing his will is having no other gods before him, or creating any substitute for him, or taking him for granted. Being faithful requires that I hallow his name and honor those he has sent to be my parents, mentors, friends and colleagues. Maintaining legal speed on this roadway means that I can never take or demean another person's life. I must be faithful to him, my spouse, and anyone else with whom I have made a sacred covenant. I cannot lie, steal or desire something so much that I would place it before him in my heart.

When I swim laps, I often use this highway system as a means by which I count the laps. It stimulates fresh and sacred revelations from God to me. He is with me as I exercise my body, my mind and my spirit. He is ever refreshing my thoughts and adding to my wisdom. It never ceases to amaze me how time flies and I forget the effort I am expending when I am on the highways of meditation and prayer. It is good to be alone with him and to ponder the ways that will lead me through his Kingdom to my eternal home.

Finally, let me urge you never to cease searching for truth. Jesus said, "The truth will set you free." (John 8:31f) In the fourth chapter of John, Jesus met a Samaritan woman at Jacob's well. She wasn't well liked in the community because she had an unsavory past. She had been married five times and was promiscuous to boot, but, oddly enough, she was also a religious person. She knew her scriptures and the history of the Hebrew tradition. He, who was untouched by the sin of the world, took time to reveal some very deep stuff to this most unlikely character. In fact, they were some of the deepest thoughts that you can find in the Gospels. He told her something I firmly believe you need to know. He said, "True worshippers will worship God in spirit and in truth."

Buddha's eighth step on the pathway to peace calls for the believer to be rightly focused. Well, searching for and wrestling with truth is the *right* focus. It far outranks religious customs, provincial traditions, ecclesiastical authority and pious, wishful thinking. Be true to yourself. Discover within the precious self the truth that God reveals and all that other stuff will become insignificant.

On the night before he was crucified, Jesus made a promise to his disciples—and I hope you are one of them. He said, "If you love me, keep my commandments; and I will ask the Father to send you a Counselor, the Spirit of Truth. This promise I have made while I am with you. The Counselor, the Holy Spirit, whom the Father will send in my name will teach you all things and bring to your remembrance all that I have said." (John 14:15 and 25) Earlier in this same chapter, he assured them that he was the Way and the Truth and anyone who wants to find the knowledge of God, that is, eternal life, can do so through him.

These are solemn "deathbed" promises worthy of your constant and sincere focus, your earnest and heartfelt study and your most genuine faith. They are gifts from God through Jesus Christ. They are what counts. They are more valuable than fine art or glo-rious music or beautiful poetry or grand cathedrals or flowery rhetoric. They can't be bought with money or created by human talent. They are gifts of grace only accessed by faith; the assurance of things hoped for; the conviction of things not seen. (Hebrews11:1)

Focus, focus, focus. Listen to God who revealed himself to the world through Jesus Christ. Forget the legends and the traditions and focus on the Word of God. Make your own decisions and come to your own conclusions. Do it with much prayer. Believe me, God finds a way to get through to each of us in our own way *if* we are willing to let him and resolve to keep our focus. There is a hymn that reminds us to "Turn your eyes upon Jesus. Look full in his wonderful face. And the things of earth will grow strangely dim, in the light of his glory and grace."

I wrote a brief hymn to the tune of "Blest Be the Tie that Binds." I think it reflects what I have tried to communicate in these pages. I bring this all to an end by praying to my God, my Savior, my Friend and my Counselor . . .

I'll listen. You speak. I'll hear.

For I will to will your will.

I know I know I want to know You,

So, I'll listen. You speak. And I'll hear.